AARON COPLAND'S
Appalachian Spring

Oxford KEYNOTES

AARON COPLAND'S
Appalachian Spring

ANNEGRET FAUSER

Oxford University Press is a department of the University of Oxford. It furthers the University's objective of excellence in research, scholarship, and education by publishing worldwide. Oxford is a registered trade mark of Oxford University Press in the UK and certain other countries.

Published in the United States of America by Oxford University Press 198 Madison Avenue, New York, NY 10016, United States of America.

Library of Congress Cataloging-in-Publication Data
Names: Fauser, Annegret, author.
Title: Aaron Copland's Appalachian Spring /Annegret Fauser.
Description: New York: Oxford University Press, 2017. |
Series: Oxford keynotes | Includes bibliographical references and index.
Identifiers: LCCN 2017002716 | ISBN 9780190646875 (pbk.: alk. paper) |
ISBN 9780190646868 (hardcover: alk. paper)
Subjects: LCSH: Copland, Aaron, 1900–1990. Appalachian Spring.
Classification: LCC ML410.C756 F38 2017 | DDC 781.5/56—dc23
LC record available at https://lccn.loc.gov/2017002716

9 8 7 6 5 4 3 2 1

Paperback printed by Webcom, Inc., Canada
Hardback printed by Bridgeport National Bindery, Inc., United States of America

INTRODUCTION

Oxford Keynotes reimagines the canons of Western music for the twenty-first century. With each of its volumes dedicated to a single composition or album, the series provides an informed, critical, and provocative companion to music as artwork and experience. Books in the series explore how works of music have engaged listeners, performers, artists, and others through history and in the present. They illuminate the roles of musicians and musics in shaping Western cultures and societies, and they seek to spark discussion of ongoing transitions in contemporary musical landscapes. Each approaches its key work in a unique way, tailored to the distinct opportunities that the work presents. Targeted at performers, curious listeners, and advanced undergraduates, volumes in the series are written by expert and engaging voices in their fields, and will therefore be of significant interest to scholars and critics as well.

In selecting titles for the series, Oxford Keynotes balances two ways of defining the canons of Western music: as lists of works that critics and scholars deem to have articulated key moments in the history of the art, and as lists of works that comprise the bulk of what consumers listen to, purchase, and perform today. Often, the two lists intersect, but the overlap is imperfect. While not neglecting the first, Oxford Keynotes gives considerable weight to the second. It confronts the musicological canon with the living repertoire of performance and recording in classical, popular, jazz, and other idioms. And it seeks to expand that living repertoire through the latest musicological research.

Kevin C. Karnes
Emory University

CONTENTS

ABOUT THE COMPANION WEBSITE

Oxford University Press has created a website to accompany *Aaron Copland's Appalachian Spring* that serves as a guide to major digitized sources relating to the genesis and initial performances of *Appalachian Spring* in 1944–45. Most of these documents are preserved in the collections of the Library of Congress in Washington, DC. They are grouped in six categories: Martha Graham's scripts; Aaron Copland's sketches and rehearsal score; selected correspondence, 1942–44; selected photographs, 1944; selected newspaper clippings, 1944–45; and several other documents. As with all of the websites for Oxford Keynotes volumes, the reader is encouraged to take advantage of this valuable online information to expand their experience beyond the print book in hand.

www.oup.com/us/acas
Username: Music5
Password: Book1745

The reader is invited to explore the full catalog of Oxford Keynotes volumes on the series homepage.
www.oup.com/us/oxfordkeynotes

ACKNOWLEDGMENTS

From the outset, Martha Graham and Aaron Copland's *Appalachian Spring* was a collaborative enterprise. Much the same can be said about my research for, and writing of, this book. Colleagues across the country generously shared their time and expertise; libraries welcomed me with open arms to explore their magnificent collections; and both the University of North Carolina at Chapel Hill and the National Humanities Center (where I was an NEH Fellow) gave me that precious gift of time to complete the manuscript in 2015–16.

I am deeply grateful to the Music Division of the Library of Congress and its wonderful staff, especially Mark Horowitz, Caitlin Miller, and Raymond White, whose deep knowledge of their priceless materials has enriched my research to no end. Janine Biunno and Heidi B. Coleman, archivists of the Isamu Noguchi Foundation and Garden Museum, shared valuable documents with me and helped with the permissions. I am also grateful to Jonathan Hiam (New York Public Library) for making work so much easier in this major collection of American music. At the National Humanities Center, the director of the Library, Brooke Andrade, and her staff also helped tremendously in dealing with my often rather arcane requests.

Colleagues, friends, and students have answered numerous questions, shared their knowledge unreservedly, and listened with generous attention to my thoughts about a work whose beauty and multifaceted richness turned—for a while—into my obsession. My thanks go to Andrea Bohlman, Mark Evan Bonds, Stephanie Jordan, Emil Kang, Cary Levine, Erin K. Maher, Chérie Rivers Ndaliko, Jocelyn Neal, Marian Smith, Helena Kopchick Spencer, David VanderHamm, and Daniel Walkowitz. Janet Eilber, the artistic director of the Martha Graham Dance Company, has been a fascinating, thoughtful, and generous interlocutor who answered my innumerable queries. I am also grateful to Minou Lallemand, the artistic director of the Onium Ballet Project (Hawaii), for her unstinting help with information. My colleague Philip Vandermeer invited me to share a draft of the manuscript with his graduate seminar "Representing Musical Appalachia"; both he and the students provided valuable feedback. Thank you!

Kevin Karnes, the Keynotes series editor, has followed the genesis of the book from its very beginnings with a perfect balance of thoughtful criticism and enthusiasm. Other colleagues, too, have given the treasured gift of their time and expertise reading, and I am grateful to Marta Robertson, Larry Starr, and the anonymous reviewers for Oxford

University Press for their comments on the complete draft. I am also grateful to Jennifer Walker for typesetting the music examples, and to Barbara Norton for her expert copy-editing.

This book owes an enormous debt to my husband, Tim Carter, a peerless intellectual companion and a very generous reader. He accompanied it from the first idea to its final version, and it is dedicated to him with love and gratitude.

ARCHIVES AND SOURCES

Library of Congress, Music Division:

ACC   Aaron Copland Collection
EHC   Erick Hawkins Collection
ESCC   Elizabeth Sprague Coolidge Collection
LBC   Leonard Bernstein Collection
MGC   Martha Graham Collection

New York Public Library, Jerome Robbins Dance Division
Lincoln Kirstein Papers, *MGZMD 97

AARON COPLAND'S
Appalachian Spring

APPALACHIAN CONNOTATIONS

O Appalachian Spring! I gained the ledge;
Steep, inaccessible smile that eastwards bends . . .
Hart Crane, The Bridge *(1930)*

WE TAKE DELIGHT IN uncovering hidden truths and motives, in exposing the man behind the curtain masquerading as the Wizard of Oz, in being in on the joke played on everyone else. And so we laugh with Aaron Copland when—soon after the fact—he revealed in more than one program note and interview that the title of *Appalachian Spring,* one of the most iconic pieces of Americana, had nothing to do with either the ballet's choreography or its score. The famous reference to Appalachia was just an afterthought, Copland explained, a phrase from a poem by Hart Crane added at the last moment by the choreographer Martha Graham. In private (writing to Darius Milhaud), Copland was willing to admit to being at work on "some Americana." But he wanted his public to believe that the Americanist references were more abstract in a piece about a generic Bride and a Husbandman celebrating their new life together in a stylized pastoral valley, supported by a wise Pioneer Woman, and a Revivalist Preacher with his flock of four Followers. Just as important as the score and its choreography, Isamu Noguchi's modernist set added a cosmopolitan elegance to American rurality (Figure 0.1). Only the uninitiated might still say—as they did to Copland over and over again—that "when I see that ballet and when I hear your music I can just *see* the Appalachians and just *feel* spring."[1]

FIGURE 0.1   Set and cast for the first production of *Appalachian Spring*, Library of Congress, Coolidge Auditorium, October 1944, photographer unknown. Library of Congress, Music Division, Elizabeth Sprague Coolidge Collection.

    AARON COPLAND'S *APPALACHIAN SPRING*

Martha Graham never disavowed the regional association. But Copland's public uncoupling of the work from its title, thereby removing any whiff of hillbilly folksiness from his score, was a smart move. Indeed, it was not until four weeks before the premiere of the ballet, on October 30, 1944, at the Library of Congress in Washington, D.C., that Martha Graham announced its name (or so it seems). It appeared first in a letter dated October 3 wherein Erick Hawkins—Graham's collaborator, dance partner, and, later, husband—informed the organizers of the premiere that they should use *Appalachian Spring* in their press release. "*My* title," Copland emphasized, "was always *Ballet for Martha*, and it became the subtitle of *Appalachian Spring*."[2]

Thus liberated from Appalachian specificity, the score, choreography, and stage set became sites for reconfiguration as expressions of modernist Americanism. In the past decade, for example, the sound world of *Appalachian Spring* has been evoked across the spectrum of American politics. John Williams's *Air and Simple Gifts* was performed at the inauguration of President Barack Obama in January 2009; a close paraphrase of the famous score accompanied Texas Governor Rick Perry's ill-fated homophobic campaign advertisement in December 2011. Meanwhile, in 1985 Noguchi produced an edition of six bronze casts of the onstage rocking chair, which, even in functional plywood, had the quality of a modernist sculpture (Figure 0.2). Such reconfigurations have served the ballet and its creators exceedingly well, all the more so as, over time, they distilled the work into its individual components of score, choreography, and set. The more abstract the work appeared, the less collective and contextually specific it seemed to be.

FIGURE 0.2   Isamu Noguchi, *Appalachian Spring: Rocking Chair*, bronze,
1944–85, Isamu Noguchi Foundation and Garden Museum.
© 2017 The Isamu Noguchi Foundation and Garden Museum,
New York/Artists Rights Society (ARS), New York.

HISTORICAL CONTEXT OF THE WORK

Appalachian Spring is not as removed from Appalachia as Copland and later commentators would have it, given the role the region played not only in the American imagination of the 1940s but also in the work's genesis, since references to it abounded both in Graham's scenarios and in her correspondence with Copland. Nor can the ballet be divorced from other cultural contexts of its creation, such as World War II, when the United States fought on the side of the Allies and was shaping its image accordingly. Cold War politics then molded the work's postwar reception at home as well as abroad, playing on the trope of Appalachian regionalism despite its creators' insistence on the work's abstract character. Indeed, regionalist identity constitutes an intrinsic quality that permeates both the ballet's creation and its reception.[3]

The work's genesis was marked by cultural and political shifts even during the two years of its gestation. Commissioned by the Elizabeth Sprague Coolidge Foundation in July 1942 as one of a pair of dance pieces, it was to be performed originally in October 1943 as part of the annual chamber-music festival at the Library of Congress. Graham straightaway sent Copland a scenario with the title "Daughter of Colchis," a Victorian psychodrama set in New England. The composer found the plot unappealing, however, and asked for a different script more akin in tone to *Our Town*, a film for which he had written the score in 1940. Ten months later, in May 1943, Graham's second scenario, this time an American Civil War drama titled "House of Victory," reached Copland in Hollywood, where he was working on the music for *The North Star*, Samuel Goldwyn's film about the German invasion of Ukraine. The composer liked the new plot better and started composing, but he asked for revisions, which Graham sent in July 1943. Copland agreed to this version and continued with the ballet, only to be interrupted by the film score, which then needed his full attention. Given that by August neither Copland nor the Mexican composer Carlos Chávez—who was to provide the music for the second ballet—were anywhere close to completing their scores, the planned premieres were canceled until further notice. To salvage things, Graham and Coolidge agreed to a different line-up: in addition to the Copland piece, there would be two others, one by Paul Hindemith and another by Darius Milhaud. Meanwhile Copland returned from Hollywood and brought with him the first part of his score. He met with Graham in New York, playing it for her on the piano in late October. By January 1944 about half of the music was completed and in Graham's hands. Copland had finished the composition by mid-June and started orchestrating. The premiere was now set for October 1944 to celebrate Coolidge's eightieth birthday. During that time Graham chose Isamu Noguchi—with whom she had collaborated earlier, in 1935, on *Frontier*—to do the sets for all three ballets, and Edythe Gilford for the costumes. By October 3 Graham had settled on *Appalachian Spring* as the final title for the work, which was then premiered, together with *Mirror Before Me* (Hindemith) and *Imagined Wing* (Milhaud), on October 30, to great public and critical acclaim.[4]

Copland saw the ballet for the first time at the Washington dress rehearsal and was delighted with the production. Yet he realized that "to my initial surprise, some music composed for one kind of action has been used to accompany something else." He could not have been entirely taken aback by Graham's changes, however, for a few months earlier he had explained to Milhaud in the typically pithy style he used in letters among friends: "My work is written to a libretto she gave me—some Americana. Doesn't matter much what the subject is—she always turns it into Grahamiana." The choreography condensed the scenario, removing much of what referred to the Civil War and its causes from the story. Instead, four archetypal characters—the Bride,

AARON COPLAND'S *APPALACHIAN SPRING*

the Husbandman, a Pioneer Woman, and a Revivalist Preacher (and his four female Followers)—were presented to the audience with barely a plot. The program book summarized it as spring being "celebrated by a man and woman building a house with joy and love and prayer; by a revivalist and his followers in their shouts of exultation; by a pioneering woman with her dreams of a promised land." Refashioned as a work about renewal and celebration, *Appalachian Spring* fit the changed landscape of late fall 1944, when the United States was starting to envision postwar reconstruction—an optimistic worldview that was a far cry from the intense anxiety two years prior, only seven months after Pearl Harbor, when the work was commissioned.[5]

Relocating *Appalachian Spring* within the context of its creation and reception provides a productive prism through which to understand its many layers of meaning and the remarkable impact on American culture since its composition and premiere. Such historically specific and culturally particular reading opens fascinating windows, too, on other questions that arise at the creative intersections of an art form as collaborative as modern dance. Despite photographs, descriptions, and other material traces, the performative ephemerality of a dance piece poses a historiographic challenge, especially when it comes to a dancer who considered her body to be an intrinsic aspect of her choreography. The work appears all the more elusive given that the performances of 1944 are, by now, overshadowed by their famous choreographic recreation for television made in 1958, and by the ballet's musical reconfiguration as an orchestral suite, with a constant presence in concert halls, on recordings, and in the broadcast media.[6]

This short book is an archaeology of sorts, not only in the sense that these pages work their way through the sediments of history to the material traces left from the original production, but also by drawing attention to the shifting ideologies that, over the years, have reconfigured the historical event and its artistic products for the particular needs of different times and circumstances. *Appalachian Spring* in 2017 is different from what it stood for just after the end of World War II. Yet in all these incarnations, the work retains, almost stubbornly, its Appalachian flavor—despite Copland's statements after the premiere—just as another world-famous ballet, Igor Stravinsky's *Rite of Spring* (1913), has never been able to shed its "Russian" associations even in the most formalist analyses of its score.

REGIONALISM DURING THE DEPRESSION AND WORLD WAR II

That this book on *Appalachian Spring* advocates becoming more attuned to the work's cultural embeddedness is no accident, given that with increased globalization, local cultural productions and regionalist identities have received renewed attention, with scholars and artists starting to reemphasize local concerns and identities. In everyday life, such terms as "locavore"—first used, according to Merriam Webster, in 2005—have become common currency. Indeed, one recent composition, *Gabriel's Guide to the 48 States* (2013), by the American composer Gabriel Kahane, stands emblematically for this return to regionalism. That work was inspired by the American Guide Series, a set of pamphlets commissioned between 1937 and 1941 by the Federal Writers Project about the (then) forty-eight states. Especially during the 1930s, America's regions became sites and symbols of progressive politics, all the more because left-wing regionalism embraced localized diversity instead of artifices representing national sameness. Folk culture—already celebrated and mythologized decades earlier by such artists as Frank Lloyd Wright, with his Prairie School style, as authentic alternatives against industrialized mass production—served the leaders of left-wing populism as proof of the inherent dignity of the common man. Such radical localism had political consequences as well. For Constance Rourke, whose work on American culture was deeply influential during the 1930s and '40s, political progress in the United States could be successful only if, as she wrote in 1933, "regional differences would seem essential for the enterprise of initiating the class struggle on any broad scale."[7]

During the Great Depression, Rourke and her fellow regionalists emphasized the pluralism of local identities whose diversity offered a hardy core of individual strengths hewn from hardship and therefore, they held, uniquely American. The cultural exigencies of World War II, however, brought a reconfiguration of the fiercely defended creed of regional difference into a patriotic, collective identity of American exceptionalism as one founded on the frontier spirit, egalitarianism in the face of shared adversity, and defense of liberty. In the 1930s New Deal folklorists such as John and Alan Lomax and Charles Seeger took pride in identifying minute variants in the folk music they collected from one county to the next. They shifted their position quite radically after Pearl Harbor, however, casting folk songs as expressions of a shared national identity. A single tune, even when its regional resonances remained, could now stand for the country as a whole. As Seeger explained, folk songs thus configured could serve as "a weapon in war." [8]

A telling example of this shift was "We Hold These Truths," a 1941 radio program commemorating the 150th anniversary of the Bill of Rights and broadcast across the four major networks shortly after Pearl Harbor. Presented by a star-studded cast that included such celebrities as Lionel Barrymore, James Stewart, and Orson Welles, it interspersed dramatized episodes about the significance of the Bill of Rights with folk songs. Yet the dramatic episodes did not feature individual figures from American regions, as they would have done only a few years earlier. Instead, the protagonist was the "Citizen" (played by Stewart), who interacted with such characters as the "Farmer," the "Mother," and the "Worker." While such abstract protagonists are familiar from left-wing political theater of the 1930s, they were here repurposed for a nationalist agenda. In lieu of a localized polyphony, the Citizen exhorted his fellow Americans to adopt "a mighty unison to prosecute a war." [9]

This turn to folkloric generalization became a distinctive trend during the war years. In Agnes de Mille and Aaron Copland's ballet, *Rodeo* (1942), the characters are identified simply—for example, as an American Cowgirl, a Head Wrangler, or a Champion Roper. Such abstractions were not unusual for ballets and modern dance per se, but when

combined with a folksy plot that would have traditionally called for an emphasis on particularity, they become
remarkable. In Copland's earlier ballet *Billy the Kid* (1938),
for instance, the protagonist and his immediate entourage
were far more individualized in Eugene Loring's scenario
and choreography, and the score carefully foregrounded
matching folkloric material. After the war broke out, by
contrast, even on Broadway such a regionally titled show as
Rodgers and Hammerstein's *Oklahoma!* (1943) proclaimed
that "The Farmer and the Cowman must be friends," and
while Laurie, Curly, Aunt Eller, and Jud have their names,
their curious lack of personal histories fits the wartime
shift to a theater of concepts. Even Oklahoma—ostensibly
the setting of the musical play—is inconspicuous in terms
of its locality: while the wind may be sweeping down the
plains and the prairie blooms in June, it is first and foremost a "grand" land that melds the "brand new state" with
the nation as a whole.[10]

Appalachian Spring crystallizes these developments
of nationalized regionalism in a fascinating manner, for
it started out with a scenario that related the plot to John
Brown's raid on Harper's Ferry just before the Civil War.
Graham's reference to John Brown was no accident, given
the abolitionist's central role in a 1938 scenario by her close
friend and confidant, Lincoln Kirstein, titled "Memorial
Day: Dances for a Democracy in Crisis," for which Copland
was slated to write the music. Graham knew this unpro-
duced scenario well and admired it profoundly. The specificity of the Appalachian location in both Kirstein's and
Graham's scenarios was in tune with other artists and writers who linked the emancipation struggle to that particular

region, not least W. E. B. Du Bois, who in his biography of John Brown identified "the great Appalachian range and its abutting mountains" as a "comparatively safe route to freedom." Indeed, through the mediation of such poets as Hart Crane—highly appreciated by Kirstein, Graham, Copland, and Hawkins—Appalachia connoted not so much a folksy southern mountain culture as the Civil War struggle at a frontier not simply between East and West, but also between North and South. This Appalachia was an urban invention that drew on its symbolic power to stand in for the nation in its struggles during the 1930s and then again during World War II. Furthermore, for artists at the progressive end of the political spectrum, keenly interested in cultural events unfolding in the USSR, the evocation of folk culture and its implied regionalism as a political tool had become legitimized through its adoption in Soviet Socialist Realism as the art of the people.[11]

But if *Appalachian Spring* started with a specific historical and local setting, the two years between its inception in July 1942 and its completion in October 1944 brought other elements into play. Graham's *Deaths and Entrances* (1943), to a score by Hunter Jones, pulled away from the more specific plots of her earlier pieces such as *American Document* (1938)—which drew on the Declaration of Independence, the Emancipation Proclamation, and other such texts—while Copland began his more abstract Violin Sonata (1943) soon after *Rodeo*. Like Graham, Copland was increasingly dealing with issues of identity in other ways as well. He found himself in a strangely challenging environment for most of 1943 when composing what he called his "Russian" score for *The North Star* (1943), a high-budget motion picture on the German invasion of Ukraine in 1941. A figure who epitomized "the all-American composer in our midst" found himself now wrestling publicly with a transatlantic ancestry (his family had its roots in Lithuania) that was often silently implied but rarely explicitly foregrounded. Added to this already complex mix was Copland's Jewishness, his left-wing politics, and his homosexuality which—though not paraded openly—was not hidden either. None of this made him any less "American," but it added layers that needed careful negotiation.[12]

These layers meshed with a reception history that started with a whimper when the press release for the premiere was delayed to the point of being ineffective. It gained much greater traction after Copland's Pulitzer Prize for the score, on May 7, 1945, and the first performance in New York on May 14, six months after the Washington premiere. Despite Copland's efforts to the contrary, critics were now quick to discuss the regional flavor both of the score and of the choreography. Even Noguchi's stage design was seen through a parochial lens, as when Margaret Lloyd, the well-known dance critic of the *Christian Science Monitor*, explained that the décor "suggests a small house in the wilderness, with front steps and a single rocking-chair to make it home. There's a side porch bench that in due course serves for a semblance of church service, and a fence that indicates pastures and woodlands—all America—beyond." After Graham took the ballet on tour, first through the United States and later to Europe and Asia, the slippage between Appalachia and America came to be recast through Copland's music and Noguchi's set design: instead of a regional identity, the work now carried a cultural one through the Shaker community evoked in Copland's quotation of "Simple Gifts" and Noguchi's rocking chair. Appalachia, too, gained new connotations. Soon Graham's use of the title was considered justified not only because of Hart Crane's poem but also because, as an article on the occasion of the television broadcast in January 1959 claimed, "the word 'Appalachian' comes from an early Indian word for 'new world.'" The greater the distance from the work's premiere, the more blurred its various components became in the reception of *Appalachian Spring*.[13]

My book parses the history of the dance piece in five chapters, tracing the events that led to the first performance of *Appalachian Spring* on the stage of the Coolidge Auditorium in the Library of Congress on a Monday evening in the final year of World War II, and then onward to its emergence as one of the best-loved works in the American musical canon. Chapters 1 and 2 tell the story of the work's genesis, not so much (as has been done so often) by focusing on one of the two protagonists of the story—either Copland or Graham—but rather by integrating them into a narrative that also involves others in the production, such as Noguchi, Hawkins, and Merce Cummingham, whose interplay was far more contrapuntal than was later assumed. Chapter 3 covers *Appalachian Spring* as it was performed in 1944–45 and as Graham "reworked it" (as she wrote to Copland in May 1945) after discussions with the composer for the New York premiere. Chapter 4 begins when the curtain fell after these first performances and explores how contemporary audiences engaged with *Appalachian Spring* as a modern-dance piece about America while the nation emerged from World War II. Chapter 5 follows the ballet as it left the stage and entered the critical and popular imaginations in both national and global terms, largely by way of Copland's score. Putting the dance, and even Appalachia, back into *Appalachian Spring* matters, we shall see. But with or without them, the work's status as an iconic symbol of a nation remains assured.

CHAPTER 1

A COMMISSION AND ITS CONTEXT

And if dance be the answer, dance!
William Carlos Williams, "War, the Destroyer!" (1942)

APPALACHIAN SPRING WAS CREATED as a dance piece about war, during war. Dance, Martha Graham claimed in 1942, was life affirming, "a definite warm living thing in the face of so much that is not." Dance, the poet William Carlos Williams wrote that same year in a poem dedicated to Graham, was a positive counterforce to the "blooming terror" of war. And together with Aaron Copland, the choreographer worked hard over two years—between 1942 and 1944—to achieve "a gentleness without sentimentality and a sense of the universal without being symbolic" by touching on the subject "so lightly," as she wrote to the composer, "that it will have none of the war as such in it." It was to be a universal piece about war and about how war related to personal sacrifice, courage, love, and hate—all words Graham used to explain the plot to Copland in late spring 1943 when she described her scenario's meaning to the composer. When *Appalachian Spring* was premiered on October 30, 1944, on the stage of the Coolidge Auditorium of the Library of Congress in Washington, D.C., the two years of its gestation had generated numerous layers of artistic decisions—and even indecision—not only about war but also about broader issues of national, gender, and ethnic identities in 1940s America that saturated the work's very fabric, even though on the surface its innocuous plot about a couple's young love seems far removed from the horrors of World War II.[1]

Appalachian Spring was a difficult piece to write both for the composer and for the choreographer. "I have really had a hard time with this, simple as it seems," Graham wrote to Copland in May 1943 about the first version of her script. She described it as faulty and having a weak ending, yet declared two months later, in July, that she was "not lost completely although I have almost been lost in the writing of this piece." Only in September of that year was she able to assure the composer that she was finally satisfied—for now—with the latest version of her script. In between, she worried about a scene early in the piece: had Copland already written the music?—perhaps it would be better to cut it entirely. Meanwhile the composer got stuck too, confessing to Graham in July 1943: "I was going well for a while, and then suddenly got bogged down. I don't know why. Your new script has been a help, and I hope to get started again."[2]

While outside complications contributed to the long gestation of *Appalachian Spring*, the rich corpus of archival remnants tells a fascinating story about the intrinsic challenges of the project and its artistic parameters, which stood in the way of what had seemed at first an easy commission to complete. Instead, the work's creators battled with a piece whose subject matter, musical style, choreography, and staging took numerous detours on its way to the Coolidge Auditorium. From the start the project was marked by twists and turns: at first the companion piece to *Appalachian Spring* was to be written by the Brazilian composer Heitor Villa-Lobos, rather than Carlos Chávez. Then Graham had to come up with a new scenario for Copland, one she titled "House of Victory." As we will see, she drew on a range of intertexts, such as Lincoln Kirstein's "Memorial Day," to create the script of what would eventually become her final and best-known piece of Americana.

LEADING UP TO THE COMMISSION

From the very first, the project that would yield *Appalachian Spring* was cast in terms of Americanism and national culture. It started with a letter that Erick Hawkins, a dancer and choreographer who had joined Graham's company in 1939, wrote to Elizabeth Sprague Coolidge in May 1942. He asked the well-known patron of the arts—who had earlier commissioned Igor Stravinsky's *Apollon Musagète* (1928) to choreography by Adolph Bolm—to turn her mind to Graham, "one of the great creative artists of America," who deserved to collaborate with a "first-rank composer" like Copland. Commissioning such a score for Graham, Hawkins's letter implied, was a patriotic act. Coolidge found the idea very attractive, though she hesitated at first because of the costs associated with a staged production.

By mid-June, however, she had already contacted a number of composers about the assignment, including Vittorio Rieti and Bernard Wagenaar. After meeting with Graham and Hawkins in Washington, she agreed that Copland and, perhaps, Villa-Lobos might make a good pair of composers to create the music for an evening of modern dances. Hawkins reported back to Coolidge that the commission gave Graham "an absolutely new lease on things. She has been a completely different woman since … I can't wait to see what will come out of the collaboration with Copland and Villa-Lobos!"[3]

When Coolidge pointed out that the war made a collaboration with Villa-Lobos somewhat of a logistical impossibility, Graham tried to convince her that this association might offer not only a fascinating "dance possibility" with a unique regionalist flavor but also a propaganda coup. Evoking the famous episode in 1941 when the score of Dmitri Shostakovich's Symphony No. 7 ("Leningrad") was flown out on microfilm from the Soviet Union to the Western Allies via Tehran, Graham presented her long-distance collaboration with Villa-Lobos as leading to "the use probably of microfilm to transport the score" from São Paulo to Washington. Thus the challenge of a transcontinental collaboration would turn Graham's and Villa-Lobos's new ballet into a pan-American counterpart to the most famous wartime composition to date, which had just received its U.S. premiere in Arturo Toscanini's famous NBC broadcast in July 1942. In the end, however, Coolidge commissioned the second score from Chávez rather than Villa-Lobos.[4]

At this point Copland was fully immersed in wartime activities, whether in terms of his unsettled draft status (his military papers had just gone missing after they were sent to the Army's Special Services in September), his work as a music advisor for the State Department, or his contributions as a composer. His first major composition responding to the U.S. entry into the war—*Lincoln Portrait*, for narrator and orchestra—had recently been premiered on May 14, 1942. The piece was based on texts by Abraham Lincoln, culminating in the final lines of the Gettysburg Address, the words perhaps most often quoted during World War II. In late August that year—about a month after the Coolidge commission—Copland received a letter from Eugene Goossens, who asked for a fanfare for the Cincinnati Symphony Orchestra. This would become *Fanfare for the Common Man*, completed in November 1942 and premiered the following March. Closer to his meeting with Graham about their new work, however, was the first performance of his latest ballet. On October 16, the Ballet Russe de Monte Carlo premiered *Rodeo* to choreography by Agnes de Mille. In a letter to Benjamin Britten, Copland described it as a "frothy ballet . . . on the usual wildwest subject—full of square dances and Scotch tunes and the like." The result was a piece whose Americanist subject led critics to proclaim it "the kind of ballet that Mark Twain might have written if his mind had run to ballets." The ballet and its resulting concert suite only added to Copland's growing reputation as a—if not the—leading contemporary composer in the United States.[5]

Rodeo's tight score seamlessly blended the cowboy vernacular with modernist techniques, encapsulating the American frontier myth in an accessible musical idiom that nonetheless laid claim to aesthetic significance. Copland made this point unequivocally in a 1943 letter to the music critic and composer Arthur Berger, in which he pointed out that "musical naturalness" in no way stood in opposition to the creation of "great" works. Indeed, for Copland, the war crystallized questions of musical identity that had their roots in the 1930s, when his allegiance to the political left merged with a populist discourse that located artistic authenticity in the expression of local, common folk, whether historic or contemporary. For example, in *The Second Hurricane,* a 1937 school opera written for the Henry Street Settlement, the composer inserted the historical tune "The Capture of Burgoyne," which he had found in S. Foster Damon's collection *Old American Songs* (1936), even though the opera dealt with a quite different, more modern subject. Yet Copland's straightforward reference to the vernacular, in terms both of style and of idiom, became increasingly problematic. While the adoption of folk art as a valid strain of Socialist Realism legitimized its use on the side of the Popular Front, its prominent place in fascist culture made it an ideologically contested ground. Not for nothing did Copland's friend and collaborator Roger Sessions warn his fellow American composers in 1940 about "quasi-fascist attitudes" that foregrounded the expression of "national feeling" and sought to establish "an American style."[6]

In the 1930s Copland's folkloric modernism could be justified not just on Popular Front grounds but also as creating a progressive counterworld against the essentialist nationalism and anti-Semitism of Nazi Germany: as a left-wing Jew, he was high on the list of composers banned in that country (beginning in 1935). But by 1942, and with so strongly marked a piece as *Rodeo*, this contrary position had lost its legitimacy in the face of the nationalist instrumentalizing of folk-inspired art on both sides of the divide. Indeed, when the dancer Ted Shawn heard Copland's score for *Rodeo* in 1942, he put his finger exactly on the negative side of nationalism when he exclaimed that "it's because of music like that that we are having war." When Copland met with Graham the week after its premiere, and despite its success, he was clearly in search of a different kind of dance project, one that connected progressive politics with American values and current wartime exigencies in another way.[7]

For her part, Graham too was shifting gears, moving into the artistic mainstream as the embodiment of American modern dance. Until the 1930s modern dance and ballet were seen as two distinct art forms in the United States: one founded on the highly formalized and disciplined European ballet schools, especially those of Imperial Russia, the other presenting a modern alternative, rooted in gestural expressivity and artistic individuality, that some viewed as particularly American, despite its cosmopolitan networks. If ballet—with its connection to the opera house—stood at the center of theater, then modern dance evolved in the alternative circuits of colleges, concert performance, and community spaces. Although Graham had become one of the celebrities of modern dance, she was far from mainstream until about 1938, when she created *American Document*, a work built on such foundational documents of the United States as the Declaration of Independence and the Gettysburg Address. By integrating the spoken word with her choreography, Graham brought elements of politically inspired pageants into modern dance. The work was a great success that, through national tours in 1939 and subsequent years, reached a coast-to-coast audience in ways modern dance had not done before. While *American Document* continued a series of choreographies that engaged with American history and identity—from *Primitive Mysteries* (1931) and *Frontier* (1935) to *American Lyric* (1937)—its perspective differed from the social critique of her earlier dance pieces. *American Document* presented a positive vision of democracy and emancipation, a conscious evocation of, as Graham said in a 1938 interview with the *Daily Worker*, "rights we have but may not avail ourselves of." With *American Document*, Graham had created a work whose politics were deliberately national in scope, just as John Latouche and Earl Robinson did with *Ballad for Americans* (1939) a year later. After Pearl Harbor, this call for democracy could easily be recast in counterpoint to Nazi ideology, as when, in September 1942, *Theatre Arts* published the libretto of *American Document* with the comment that Graham "had been listening to the vicious and terrifying words sent over the air from the Axis countries. It occurred to her that our own country— our democracy—has words, too, with power to hearten men and move them to action." What had started out as a left-wing evocation of democratic values from an antifascist artist had been transformed, through the outbreak of the war, into a nationalist call to arms.[8]

    AARON COPLAND'S *APPALACHIAN SPRING*

American Document was a watershed work in other respects as well, for it brought into Graham's professional and personal circles the first male dancer to join her company, Erick Hawkins. Having come late to dance (following a degree from Harvard in ancient Greek civilization), he studied at Georges Balanchine's School of American Ballet from 1933 onwards. Together with Eugene Loring and Lew Christensen, he was one of three young American dancers and choreographers whom the writer and impresario Lincoln Kirstein brought into the fold of his newly founded Ballet Caravan in 1936, a troupe dedicated to fostering American ballet. Hawkins joined Graham at Bennington College for the summer of 1938 to learn more about modern dance, where she choreographed a major part—including an important solo—for him in *American Document*. Until 1939, when he became an official member of Graham's dance company, his affiliation remained with the Ballet Caravan, dancing in Copland and Loring's *Billy the Kid* in 1938 and 1939. Both Kirstein and Hawkins played major roles in Graham's life as lovers, friends, inspiration, and support; eventually—and after a difficult break-up in 1946—Graham married Hawkins in 1948. Indeed, Kirstein and Hawkins each had a part in the creation of *Appalachian Spring*, one through earlier influences, the other as her constant companion.[9]

THE DEVELOPMENT OF GRAHAM'S SCENARIO

The fall of 1942, when the collaboration between Graham and Copland for *Appalachian Spring* began in earnest, was a turning point both for the composer and for the choreographer. They met in New York the week after the premiere of *Rodeo*, and judging from the traces in the surviving documents, their conversation navigated some rocky ground. Graham had wanted to make the new work a Medea story, an idea Copland flat-out rejected. For his part, Copland had been looking to compose "a Shaker one acter" since 1941 and might have tried convincing Graham to turn their project into that. Although her next scenario did indeed mention a Shaker rocking chair as a prop, the choreographer did not seem particularly taken with the idea of a Shaker-centered piece as such. There was, however, an earlier project with which Copland and Graham both had been associated in 1938–39, one that fit their artistic and political project as progressive Americanists, and one that—like *Lincoln Portrait* and *American Document*—connected the current political context with key texts of American history. Lincoln Kirstein's ballet scenario "Memorial Day: Dances for a Democracy in Crisis" never reached fruition, but it was to have clear echoes in *Appalachian Spring*. Whether Copland and Graham recalled that project in their conversation or— more likely—whether Graham turned to it as a result of their discussion, "Memorial Day" seems to have helped put things on a better track. Soon after their meeting Hawkins told Coolidge that "it was all set between them to go ahead" and that Graham was "already feeling her way, into the idea I mean." In early November Graham told Copland that she was "working on an idea which I hope you may like better than the script you have." It would take Graham another six months, however, to give her thoughts some near-final form.[10]

"Memorial Day" was to be "a drama for dancers," Kirstein explained, set between 1858 and 1865. As he pointed out, the work had "certain obvious parallels with our present," presenting "the background, causes, acts and results of a civil conflict." It also included the spoken word, quoting from, among others, Walt Whitman and Abraham Lincoln. This scenario was obviously an artistic response to the Memorial Day Massacre on May 30, 1937, when Chicago police killed ten unarmed protesters during the so-called Little Steel Strike. Its music would be by none other than Copland, whose detailed "musical synopsis" called for brass band, Hammond organ, and percussion (as well as optional fifes or flutes), an instrumentation familiar from outdoor dramas. Lew Christensen was slated to be the stage director, and the choreography was to be split among Kirstein's "chosen three" from the Ballet Caravan: Christensen, Hawkins, and Loring. The first part of the ballet was set in the North as an open-air picnic; the second, in the South as an indoor ball; and the third was a Memorial Day celebration. Interspersed throughout were episodes about a fugitive slave; the Harper's Ferry raid, trial, and execution of John Brown (to be choreographed and danced by Hawkins); a play within a play representing *Uncle Tom's Cabin*; scenes from a Civil War encampment; and a home broken by the war—represented only by "the shape of a doorway" and a table.[11]

Kirstein discussed "Memorial Day" with Graham as he developed the idea and later sent her the completed scenario, which he had put together for potential backers and who might include, he said, a trade union representing "an industry gaining its materials from the south which are manufactured in the north." In an undated letter that seems to have been written either in late 1938 or early in 1939, Graham commented that "just seeing your outlines etc. for 'Memorial Day' have taught me the value of orderly & consummated thought. I hope something like this goes into the program books." She contrasted his scenario with *American Document*—which she found wanting in comparison—yet "it is important that people hear what it says again—even more important than when I did it. And it is terribly important that 'Memorial Day' be done with its final accent of courage." Unfortunately, as Graham pointed out, backers were hard to find, and in the end, "Memorial Day" remained just a scenario.[12]

When Graham searched for a plot that would please Copland, two other factors besides the composer's own involvement in the abandoned Kirstein project may well have brought it into play: the presence of Hawkins, who during those years was consumed with the creation of another John Brown ballet; and the repeated radio broadcasts, in 1942 and 1943, of Copland's *Lincoln Portrait*, a work with which both Hawkins and Graham were utterly taken. And so for her new project with Copland, Graham wrote a scenario set during the Civil War that comprised episodes of a fugitive slave and a play within a play representing *Uncle Tom's Cabin*; that featured "the kind of man that became the abolitionist, the John Brown"; that presented a home through "the frame of a doorway"; and that staged both a "Day of War" and a final apotheosis, the "Time of Return." Yet Graham turned Kirstein's "Memorial Day" scenario into something more general and more abstract by way of her four main characters: the Mother, the Daughter, the Citizen, and the Fugitive. Her views of Copland's recent compositions—particularly *Quiet City* and *Lincoln Portrait*—also moved away from the folkloric. Although Copland did cite actual folk material, Graham characterized *City* and *Portrait* as "so utterly beautiful in having been woven on this country's loom without seeming to use any folk material really."[13]

The plot Graham had developed for her new scenario, titled "House of Victory," tells the story of a couple's courtship and wedding (with a big charivari), followed by an interlude staging the beginning of their life in their community. Their idyll is interrupted first by an old-fashioned showboat stage on which "crucial scenes" from *Uncle Tom's Cabin* are performed, and then by the Fugitive, an escaped slave whom the Mother hides behind her skirts. This episode is followed by a segment set during the Civil War and meant to represent the entire four years of the conflict, but—as Graham explains—"it is the state of war at any time." The Husband leaves, only to return in the final scene, configured as a postwar reunion, celebration, and final contemplation, the outline of which remains rather vague.

The entire scenario is liberally interspersed with biblical quotations "because there are certain groups of people who think in Bible terms and incidents." The script also evokes a regionalist identity that merges a fictitious valley in Western Pennsylvania with Appalachia's Harper's Ferry. Indeed, Graham conjures Appalachia not only through her repeated references to John Brown but also by comparing the Citizen to the mountain man Davy Crockett. Despite such specificity, however, the new piece was simply "a legend of living in the *American place*." Just as the Civil War stood for all war, including the current one, the Appalachian village embodied the nation as a whole.

Graham's scenario has an unsettled quality to it, suspended somewhere between the Popular Front aesthetics of the 1930s and contemporary wartime nativism. Clearly, Copland's rejection of the original Medea scenario had thrown her for a loop, and so it makes sense that she used "Memorial Day" and *Lincoln Portrait* as a new points of departure, given their connection to the composer. But Graham's scenario reveals also another intertext: Rodgers and Hammerstein's musical play *Oklahoma!*, which had its New York premiere on March 31, 1943, the very time when Graham wrote her "House of Victory" script. She was familiar with the show and especially, of course, the choreography of its dance sequences by her close friend, Agnes de Mille. Graham's description of the set for "House of Victory" evokes the one by Lemuel Ayers for *Oklahoma!*, with its house and fence and rocking chair on the porch. Most striking, however, is her conception of the wedding celebration, which places the Daughter and the Citizen inside the house while "the party outside develops into an old fashioned chivari (charivari)." Charivaris had a long tradition, rooted in the Middle Ages, of serenading a newlywed couple on their wedding night in a noisy, riotous manner that often involved banging on pots and pans and other discordant devices. Though Graham spells the term differently from Hammerstein, her phonetic rendering of "shivoree" (as it was called in *Oklahoma!*)—with the conventional spelling in brackets—makes the reference apparent. Indeed, this scene comes straight from the finale of *Oklahoma!*, where it sticks out as a strange, archaic ritual that might well have caught Graham's attention as something taking place "in the out districts of this country" and thus appropriate for her new Americanist work.[14]

Graham completed the "House of Victory" scenario in late April 1943 and sent it to Copland on May 16. She must have been aware of its somewhat incongruous quality because she admitted—with rhetorical flair—to approaching him "with fear and trembling on two accounts; one is lateness of this and the other is ... will you like it at all and will it be something you can work with." By then Copland had left the East Coast for an eight-month stay in Hollywood to work on his film score for *The North Star*. Given the geographic dispersion of the main characters, business now had to be done by mail, with Copland on the West Coast, Graham in New York and Bennington, and Harold Spivacke—the musicologist who, as chief of the Music Division of the Library of Congress, was responsible for the practical aspects of the Coolidge commission—in Washington. Even though Graham—with her peripatetic existence at the time—did not keep much of the correspondence she received (Copland's letters to her are lost), the other players were more careful with their archives, and so we have an unusually rich cache of documents chronicling the debates and decisions involved as the project moved forward.[15]

Within days of obtaining the scenario, Copland wrote back to Graham. He liked her overall idea, but he also had plenty to criticize, especially the second part, from the *Uncle Tom* episode onward. As one can infer from Graham's response, on May 29, the composer found the play within a play distracting and her treatment of the Civil War somewhat heavy-handed. He also seems to have queried the wisdom—or even appropriateness—of her biblical quotations. Graham promised that she would rework her scenario in accordance with his requests, especially "from the beginning of the Episode on." But she took another six weeks to come up with a version that excised the *Uncle Tom* episode, adding instead an Indian Girl, a Pocahontas figure modeled, as she wrote, on "the use that Hart Crane made of her" in his famous poem *The Bridge*, a line of which would eventually yield the title of *Appalachian Spring*. In the revised scenario, Graham tried to integrate the Girl as embodying the nation, "like a tree or a rock in her relationship to the place": she "is in the names of our cities and rivers." But in this version, too, the choreographer's vision remained bogged down in details as they related to the Civil War Appalachia of John Brown. As she confessed to Copland: "I realize anew how difficult it is to use the American material, and it has not shaped well to my touch." Yet she sent it off, and despite his misgivings about the addition of the Indian Girl and Graham's continued insistence on biblical verses, Copland approved the second scenario officially in mid-July. In effect, he had already started composing music for that part of "House of Victory" that was to his liking: the opening through to the wedding charivari. Now, however, he became sidetracked by a different project—*The North Star*—while Graham continued to tinker with her recalcitrant scenario, until she, too, turned to a different project later in the fall.[16]

CHAPTER 2

THE CREATION OF A DANCE PIECE

To be hybrid anticipates the future.
This is America. The nation of all nationalities.
Isamu Noguchi, "I Become a Nisei" (1942)

THE MAKING OF *APPALACHIAN SPRING* involved ever-widening circles of collaborators whose artistic and personal agendas left their marks on the work. This was the case in particular with Aaron Copland and Isamu Noguchi, both of whom also faced challenges to their senses of self that were brought on by the war. These artists, who had been so strongly involved in the American avant-garde of the 1930s, now encountered questions about their national identities—more subtly in the case of Copland, but very directly so far as Noguchi was concerned. In either case, *Appalachian Spring*, with its Americana appeal, proved the perfect vehicle for them to position themselves within American art during World War II. As the production headed toward its premiere, other collaborators contributed important elements to the work's unique character as well.

THE SCORE AND ITS CONTEXT

When Copland received Graham's first scenario for *Appalachian Spring* in May 1943 (titled "House of Victory"), he had been in Hollywood for three months, immersed in one of the most expensive film productions in recent history: *The North Star*. Based on a script by Lillian Hellman—notorious not only as a prominent left-wing writer but also as the former director of the Federal Theatre Project—the film was set in 1941 and followed the inhabitants of a village in Ukraine through the course of the German invasion. It was a call to arms in support of the Soviet Union, a nation still regarded with suspicion in the United States notwithstanding its new status as an ally against the Axis powers. The story begins with the pastoral idyll of an intact rural community, visually not that different from 1940s movie depictions of Midwestern farms. After showing the German destruction and atrocities during the invasion, it ends with the heroic actions of guerilla fighters and a vision of a peaceful future in a free world, despite the destruction of the village. The film was a Hollywood production about an idealized ally, mediating Soviet heroism for an American audience through its screenplay, camerawork, and narrative gesture, and with American actors representing their Ukrainian characters without any foreign accent (though Erich von Stroheim was cast as one major German character, a doctor harvesting the blood of the village children).

Music needed to contribute to this idealized view of the nation's new ally, and with Copland, Samuel Goldwyn brought to the production a major American composer with roots in the former Russian empire: both of his parents had emigrated from Lithuania (an area subsumed under the designation "Russian" by Copland's American contemporaries). Ira Gershwin, another second-generation Russian Jew, wrote the lyrics for the songs performed in the movie. The film called for a substantial amount of music, from diegetic peasant dances and songs to the underscoring of battle scenes. Together Copland and Gershwin created a soundscape at once Russian and American, folkloric and modernist. As Copland put it in a short text written right after he completed the score: "In general, guided by the fact that American actors were performing without attempting Russian accents, I determined on using a style that would merely suggest, without overemphasizing, the Russian element." The press inscribed this sonic hybridity into the body of the composer himself, however, when it portrayed Copland as "the all-American composer in our midst," who, despite the fact that his "parents were born in Russia ... writes music characterized by the one word 'Yankee.'" Drawing on essentialist notions of national identity, the report cast Copland's American sound not as a consequence of his ancestry but as something he had achieved despite his Russian roots. And not only did he conduct "research into the folk music of his ancestors," the *Los Angeles Times* reported; "he finds himself at home in it." The composer of such Americana as *Billy the*

Kid and *Rodeo* was quickly transformed into an authentic Russian by virtue of his ancestry.[1]

The newspaper might have gushed about Copland's musical homecoming in *The North Star*, but for the composer, things were nowhere near as clear-cut in terms of the complex identity politics at work in the score. Copland emphasized that neither Russian nor Soviet songs were his most important point of reference; rather, the challenge lay in the modernist viability of the music. With this rhetorical gambit, Copland neatly sidestepped any potential alignment between his own left-wing politics and the increasingly totalitarian communism of the USSR. Composing a Hollywood score about Soviet Russia, he pointed out, "was something of the same problem Schostakovitch would have had if he had been asked to supply a score for a movie that was set in the United States." Just as American folk music and jazz might be exotic for a Shostakovich, so the use of Russian folk music was foreign to him, Copland claimed. As a modernist composer, he had the tools at his disposal to develop an appropriate idiom by starting from "actual Russian folk material," but he posited it as a compositional challenge, not a personal one. Again, he put himself on the American side of the cultural divide when he explained that "Song of the Fatherland," a Soviet song used in the movie, was "analogous to our own 'My Country 'Tis of Thee.'" And in a letter to Leonard Bernstein, Copland distinguished explicitly between his own music and "one or two interpolated numbers by real Russians."[2]

Copland's insistence on his American modernist position made ideological and political sense during World

War II, especially given how closely his Eastern European background was tied to his Jewish roots. In a country such as the United States, where the global conflict gave new credence to nativist discourse, identities that were marked as Other—whether religiously, politically, or nationally—were perceived as increasingly precarious and could potentially be used as markers for stereotyping and discrimination. Like many other Jewish artists with Eastern European backgrounds, such as Oscar Hammerstein II, Copland was cagey about his double heritage during the war years. Moreover, both his religious and his Eastern European identities carried musical signification that did not align with his vision for American music. Even as a student Copland had internalized the concepts of his teacher, Nadia Boulanger, that a composer's individuality inescapably marked his musical idiom. But judging from Copland's writing, nurture could trump nature.[3]

Musical technique, in particular, could help shape which aspect of a given personality was to be foregrounded and discipline any unwieldy tendencies. In a comment to Arthur Berger in the early 1950s, Copland distinguished between his "need to find a musical language that would have [an] American quality" and his Jewish side, "a—shall we say Hebraic—idea of the grandiose, of the dramatic and the tragic." Copland saw his American and his Jewish identities as being at odds, but he felt that by embracing the American way he could temper the religious and ethnic influences of his ancestry. A revealing passage in his later autobiography reinforces the point inasmuch as he draws a connection between his family heritage and his search for an American vernacular in music:

Both my parents were members of large families, my father being the oldest of eight children and my mother one of nine. All of my fifteen uncles and aunts were either born in the United States or brought here from abroad. Even a child could sort them out, if only because of the way they spoke—with or without a foreign accent. (I mention this detail because it may have had something to do with my later stressing the need for a specifically American speech in our serious music.)

Erasing any foreign accent was thus a key component of the composer's determination to develop an American musical vernacular.[4]

This no doubt also helps explain Copland's abhorrence of sentimentality and his view that dwelling upon irrationality and emotion was antithetical to true art. In numerous writings the composer presented objectivity, control, and clarity as markers of genuinely "American" music—all the more so around 1943, when he found himself challenged as the "Russian" composer of *The North Star*. His deliberate control becomes audible in the structure of the film's score, which is remarkable in its lucid construction and taut restraint, and in the relative absence of "folk" markers that some had viewed as characteristic of his works in the 1930s. Such a deliberate turn to classical forms can be observed also in the Sonata for Violin and Piano, written concurrently with *The North Star* in 1943. Copland spent time studying classical models as he mapped out his own composition, and while his idiom played into an American pastoral, especially in the first movement, the Sonata is a far cry from the cowboy tunes and cheeky rhythms of *Rodeo*. Nor was Copland the only composer in Hollywood at the time who turned to the sonata as a counterpoint to film-music composition: Hanns Eisler, for example, wrote his Third Sonata for Piano in 1943 while working on *Hangmen Also Die!* (1943).[5]

The formalist qualities of Copland's Violin Sonata and *The North Star* also characterize the music he wrote for Graham. In effect, Copland would draw on one of his sketches for one or other, dated February 22, 1942, as a key motive in the composition of *Appalachian Spring*, which he started in May 1943. He used it in the first part of the work, which—according to Graham's scenario—was to represent a new day, introducing the main characters one by one (Example 2.1). Furthermore, *Appalachian Spring* and *The North Star* share a surprising range of other musical idioms and expressive registers above and beyond their respective pastoral openings with similar melodic contours and rhythmic gestures in the woodwinds.

EXAMPLE 2.1   Aaron Copland, sketch, dated February 22, 1942, "used in App Spr." Transcribed from "Ballet for Martha/Rough Sketches/June 1942–June 1944," *ACC*, box 76.

Given the events in spring and summer of 1943, it was no surprise that Copland worked on both *The North Star* and *Appalachian Spring* at the same time. So far as he was concerned, the film's production schedule veered between periods of intense activity and doing nothing at all. While he waited, the composer became rather bored. As he wrote to Leonard Bernstein in late spring 1943: "Hollywood is dull dull

dull. I've written a guerilla song that everyone says is good (32 meas! Oh no—its 35!!)—even Mr. Sam Goldwyn. Wish you could have seen us playing the Internationale to him in his office." So when Graham finally sent the script for "House of Victory" in May, Copland set to work immediately, even though, as we have seen, he was still demanding revisions for the scenario's second half. Not only was he keen to get to work on the new project, but he was also acutely aware that the date originally set for the premiere (October 30, 1943) was rapidly approaching and that, once the movie was ready to be scored, he would have no time for anything else. He spent most of June on the dance piece and by mid-July had completed about a third of it. As he explained to Graham: "I have sketched out the music as far as the end of the lyric interlude. The court-ship scene is finished, but that is all that is. Everything is still rough. The opening scene, however, is almost done."[6]

Then, just as Graham sent the revised scenario—where she had deleted the *Uncle Tom's Cabin* section but added the Indian Girl—*The North Star* took over. Copland needed to provide well over an hour's worth of music in the span of about a month. At this point he suggested postponing the Graham premiere, to which she agreed through gritted teeth, though she had scant choice given that Carlos Chávez's score had not arrived either. In her official correspondence, especially with Harold Spivacke as the representative of the Elizabeth Sprague Coolidge Foundation, she remained polite, but she let loose in a letter to Erick Hawkins: "I wrote a long letter to Spivacke this morning . . . I was opposed to postponing at this time. Only in case of desperate need and after the scores were in. I think the postponement should come only if I cannot get them done and not to help the composers. I did not tell him that, however, because if we postpone the composers will postpone their finishing and that will get us nowhere." Graham was right to worry about allowing her composers the luxury of additional time to complete their music. Chávez did nothing in the end and would eventually be replaced by Paul Hindemith and Darius Milhaud. Copland, too, put the Graham commission to one side as he finished the music for *The North Star*. The film was released on November 4, 1943, in New York and brought Copland an Oscar nomination for best score.[7]

However, he returned to the composition of *Appalachian Spring* as soon as possible, perhaps even while he was still in Hollywood, for on October 22, shortly after his return to New York, he met with Graham and played for her what he had written so far. She was ecstatic, finding the music "very beautiful," as she reported to Spivacke, "clear and definite in line." By mid-January 1944 Graham had received about half of Copland's score and had started working on the choreography. She confessed to "hounding" Copland for the rest of the music but had to wait two more months for the next installment, which arrived in mid-March. From Graham's letters to Copland, it seems that this was when the composer presented her with what would become the most famous segment of his score: a Shaker tune ("Simple Gifts") and its variations. But Graham was not entirely convinced that using a Shaker melody was a good idea until she received the final score in early June, after which she conceded that the tune and its variations would "stay with people and give them great joy." After six intense weeks with the score, she wrote to Copland in August that she had become obsessed by his music. Yet it drove her also to "doing a little cursing" because it "has made me change in many places." Her scenario no longer worked with the completed score, for "it is so knit and of a completeness that it takes you in very strong hands and leads you into its own world." Graham now condensed the characters and story lines of the 1943 scenario into a tight plot. Nonetheless, its original elements as they related to rural domesticity, frontier life, and the Civil War remained an important part of the dance piece, albeit in a more abstract form, shaping the narrative of the final choreography in important ways. Moreover, the episodic nature of Graham's earlier scenario found its echo in the musical structure of the score, the modular character of which reflected not only the swift scene changes of Graham's initial plot but also the segmented configuration that Copland had developed in his recent film score.[8]

COLLABORATORS IN THE STAGING

As *Appalachian Spring* headed to the stage, the circle of co-creators widened significantly. The event was now scheduled for the eightieth-birthday celebrations of Elizabeth Sprague Coolidge, on October 30, 1944. It was combined with two more chamber-dance pieces, *Imagined Wing*, to music by Milhaud, and *Mirror Before Me*, with a score by Hindemith. With three different modern-dance pieces newly created for one evening—rather than the more usual presentation of just a single new work together with other, established ones—preparations for the premiere posed significant challenges that were exacerbated by wartime restrictions on material and manpower.

Despite Graham's annoyance with the yearlong delay, the postponement to 1944 opened up some collaborative opportunities that would have been less likely the previous year. Indeed, in 1943 the dancer Yuriko Kikuchi was still interned in a U.S. detention camp for Japanese Americans, while the production's stage designer, Isamu Noguchi, had only just been freed from his confinement in Poston, Arizona. Yuriko, as she was known, joined the Martha Graham Company soon after her release in September 1943, first as a seamstress and member of the support staff for the company. The young dancer's casting as one of the Followers in *Appalachian Spring* was her first appearance with the company onstage. She also held a leading role in *Imagined Wing*. Graham's inclusion of a Japanese American performer should probably be seen as a political act at a time when Japanese Americans were still treated as potential enemy aliens, though Yuriko was not the first Japanese American in Graham's company—Ailes Gilmour, Noguchi's sister, had danced with Graham in the 1930s. Yet the inclusion of Yuriko would also have a ripple effect when Leonard Bernstein engaged Sono Osato in 1945 for *On the Town* without even asking her to audition.[9]

Noguchi's stage design for *Appalachian Spring* (and for the other two dance pieces that evening) marked his second collaboration with Graham, after *Frontier* in 1935. She approached him in 1944—probably in late spring—after Arch Lauterer, the stage designer she had originally contracted, bowed out of the project. Hawkins claimed later that he himself was the one "responsible for Isamu's work with Martha on *Appalachian Spring*." Noguchi's style had turned toward abstraction in the wake of Pearl Harbor, seemingly stepping away from the left-wing political activism he shared with Graham and Copland during the 1930s. In 1934, for example, his sculpture *Death* presented the contorted body of an African American lynching victim. The subject matter itself was controversial, but the press's hostility toward a Japanese American, no less, daring to engage with American racism created a sensation. Noguchi's own racial identity was increasingly becoming marked as foreign and potentially hostile, and he responded by exploring forms of artistic hybridity that would inscribe his Japanese heritage into democratic American pluralism—the opposite of any Axis axiom of racial purity. The strategy was similar to that of African American writers such as Langston Hughes, who posited artistic multiplicity as a distinctly American contribution to world culture. For Noguchi, the creative solution lay in a turn toward abstraction, where Western modernism could blend with a formal language drawn from Japanese art.[10]

Three small sketches for *Appalachian Spring* show this process of cultural blending and abstraction at work (Figure 2.1). Noguchi noted that these were "study drawings at beginning for transforming Library of Congress Theater." They juxtapose a rough sketch identified as "The Noh Stage" with two versions of the stage set for *Appalachian Spring*, one showing a simple prairie house and the other presenting its abstraction into the basic geometric structure that would be the final stage design, with its sparse evocation of a frontier cabin and its porch (Figure 2.2). Noh is the revered form of classical Japanese theater, incorporating dance and music, that dates back to the fourteenth century. Hawkins made the connection explicitly (in January

  AARON COPLAND'S *APPALACHIAN SPRING*

FIGURE 2.1   Isamu Noguchi, sketches for the stage set for *Appalachian Spring*, pencil on paper, Isamu Noguchi Foundation and Garden Museum. © 2017 The Isamu Noguchi Foundation and Garden Museum, New York/Artists Rights Society (ARS), New York.

1945 to a Vassar student while touring with *Appalachian Spring*) when he related Graham's choreography to the use of "dance as employed in Japanese staging, proving that the entire emotional content of a scene can be portrayed without words and without the conventions of the theatre." For Yuriko, too, the Noh reference was self-evident. She recalled that it was "such a brilliant set" and lauded Noguchi's use "of space with the fence—it has the sense of a Japanese house with a rock garden." Yet for both Yuriko and Noguchi, the fence in *Appalachian Spring* might have carried a different, unspoken association as well: an echo of the fences that kept them confined in the camps in which they had been interned less than two years before.[11]

As Graham's domestic and dance partner, Hawkins remained strongly involved in the creation of *Appalachian*

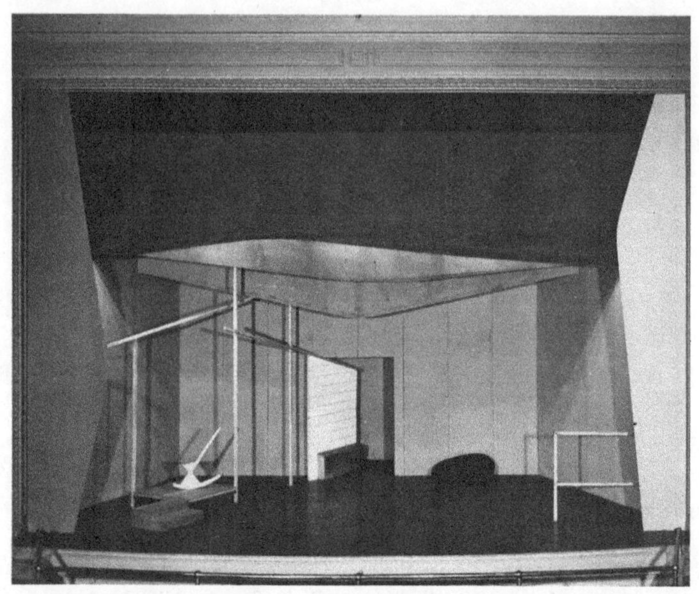

Spring. During that time his own interest as a choreographer was captured by the conception and creation of *John Brown,* a solo dance work premiered in May 1945 that combined Hawkins's performance with the recitation of historical documents relating to the abolitionist's life and death. Given that the figure of the Husbandman in the earlier *Appalachian Spring* scenarios was strongly identified with John Brown (as well as Davy Crockett), vestiges of these historical figures were present within Hawkins's character in Graham's choreography as well. Indeed, despite the many other cultural references—from Noguchi's Noh stage to Copland's Shakers—Appalachia and the Civil War remained constantly on Graham's mind during the development of the choreography, not only because Hawkins continued working on such figures as Lincoln and Brown, but also because Graham's construction of the plot had deep roots in this cultural framework. Anna Sokolow, one of Graham's dancers, recalled rather acerbically that—despite having "a 'noble feeling' for all religions"—the choreographer "didn't like her girls going to mosques or temples. She talked endlessly about the American folk roots, about Appalachia." Graham also evoked Appalachia as a point of reference when she described the dance piece in a letter to Copland as "a legend that you and I did in Appalachian."[12]

How fully imbued the final choreography was with the cultural markers of Appalachia is seen particularly in the addition of the Revivalist and his four Followers. It has become common for scholars to conflate Graham's earlier evocations of Puritans—for example, in *American Provincials* (1934) or *Letter to the World* (1940)—with the Revivalist in *Appalachian Spring*. Yet this character, with his Followers, draws on a tradition different from the Puritanism of New England: that of southern fire-and-brimstone preachers, and their ability to incite "rapt ecstasy" among their congregations. Nor was Graham choreographing the Revivalist's solos herself, as she did with the rest of *Appalachian Spring*. Rather, she gave Merce Cunningham a free hand with key moments of that role. Their collaboration drew in part on Graham's description of the Fugitive, whose music would be used for the Revivalist's major solo, and in part on the popular imaginary of southern preachers, who—as a 1955 program note explained—were "often fanatic in temper" and whose sermons evoked vividly "the imagined horrors of hell and damnation." Next to Graham's own performance, Cunningham's Revivalist dominated the choreography, much to Hawkins's chagrin: a few years later he accused Graham of having favored Cunningham at every turn, not least in *Appalachian Spring*, where "his part or performance was definitely ahead of mine."[13]

As the choreography and staging took shape over the summer and fall of 1944, practical considerations intruded on the production process, from such issues as finding stagehands who were not liable to be drafted into the armed forces to keeping the dance company afloat until the premiere. Indeed, the surviving correspondence offers a number of fascinating insights not only into the running of a modern-dance company during this period, but also into the asymmetrical relationship between patron and artist. The latter shines through with the third piece on the program, Milhaud's *Imagined Wing*. Until early April 1944, only two new works were scheduled for the Coolidge Festival: the Copland and the Hindemith (replacing Chávez). Yet, on April 25, Spivacke (acting on Coolidge's behalf) commissioned a score from Milhaud, to be delivered by July 1. Because of the tight time frame, Graham agreed to forgo her usual procedure of working from a script and would instead "compose the dances to the music." Clearly she did so under duress and in response to a specific request by Coolidge, who had taken Milhaud under her wing and used her patronage to support the French Jewish composer in exile. As Hawkins pointed out, Graham considered *Imagined Wing* "the third, additional, and less important piece," and it remained the stepchild of the event.[14]

Meanwhile, Graham's dance company was running out of money. The New York patron, Alma Morgenthau, was supposed to have financed Graham during the lead-up to the Washington premiere, but she backed out at the last minute. Hawkins asked Spivacke for a letter confirming all the details of the commission so that Graham could secure a bank loan to keep the company afloat. Spivacke obliged postehaste with a letter confirming that the Coolidge Foundation would pay Graham "the sum of $5,856 after the second performance to cover all costs connected to the preparation and presentation of these three works." He then concisely laid out the contractual obligations of both parties, which showed that Graham was responsible for providing everything for that sum, from the dancers' salaries to the sets, with the exception of the Washington stagehands, electricians, and musicians. Even in 1944, $5,856 was a modest sum. As a point of comparison at the other end of the spectrum, the most lavishly produced Broadway show of that period, Oscar Hammerstein II's *Carmen Jones* (1943), had cost had cost thirty times as much ($176,000) by the time it completed its tryouts and arrived on Broadway.[15]

That the Library of Congress covered the expense for stagehands, electricians, and musicians was clearly necessary, given the relatively high cost of unionized labor. But a number of letters reveal how strongly finances, even with those expenses defrayed, shaped artistic decisions about *Appalachian Spring*. Not only did Graham try to lower Copland's royalties from $20 per performance to $15, but she also pleaded with the composer to reduce his performing forces. After their meeting in October 1943, when Copland played his first part of the score for Graham, she wrote to Spivacke: "I have only one worry and that is the orchestration that he plans. It will sound very wonderful, I am certain, but I worry about being able to use as many different musicians." As she explained to the composer, it was "not only the expense of any player in performance, but the rehearsal difficulties" that she shied away from, especially when it came to securing so many different performers on tour. While Copland insisted on using the full contingent of thirteen players for the premiere and at major performance venues (such as the National Theatre in New York), he compromised and offered her an alternative ensemble of nine musicians when on tour by reducing the number of string players. But there were also other issues regarding the musicians: as Spivacke pointed out, the military draft made it difficult to get hold of them—even for the performance at the Library of Congress.[16]

Nonetheless, preparations for the premiere continued. Sets were built, costumes made, and lighting plans developed. At the end of September Helen Lanfer, Martha Graham's rehearsal pianist, "obtained her union card this morning in Local 802" so that she could perform at the premiere. Yet no publicity for the performance had yet been released. During September and October 1944 Spivacke and his colleagues were too busy dealing with his war-related activities for, among other things, the Joint Army and Navy Committee for Welfare and Recreation. As Copland wrote to Bernstein from Mexico in early October about his going to Washington later in the month: "Martha Graham is supposedly doing a ballet of mine that week-end! No-one has seen any public announcement of the event—nor have I—but Spivacke keeps writing it will take place, so I go on faith." Three weeks before the performance there was still no press release. "Nothing has been announced as to the subject of any of the three compositions," the *New York Times* informed its readers, "but rumor has it that the one for which Copland has written the music deals with the Shakers, and that the Hindemith piece has to do with Herodias." When Austin Wilder Management, who represented Graham, finally received the go-ahead to publicize the premiere, it was late in the game, and most critics had already committed themselves to attending a different event taking place in New York: the opening of the Ballet International's new season. And so—after a week of rehearsals in Washington—the curtain rose to an audience mainly of Washington insiders for the premiere of what would become one of the most successful works in American music and dance.[17]

CHAPTER 3

APPALACHIAN SPRING PERFORMED

Collaboration is a beautiful word,
or was until debased by the Nazis.

Jean Rosenthal, The Magic of Light *(1969)*

MARTHA GRAHAM AND HER team—from the famous lighting designer Jean Rosenthal to her house conductor, Louis Horst—came to Washington to stage the premiere of *Appalachian Spring*. It took place on October 30, 1944, in the Coolidge Auditorium of the Library of Congress, a chamber-music hall with about 480 seats, with Aaron Copland in attendance (Figure 3.1). Afterward Graham took the ballet on a successful tour of the East Coast. Because of the wartime-related entertainment boom in New York, there was a shortage of available theaters. In fact, it took half a year for Graham finally to secure the Shubert-owned National Theatre on Broadway, which seated almost 1,200. The theater was sold out when she presented a revised choreography of

Appalachian Spring there on May 14, 1945, a week after Aaron Copland had been awarded the Pulitzer Prize for its score. That same month the composer began to arrange the work as a concert suite for full orchestra. This was first heard in New York on October 4, 1945, almost a year after the Washington premiere, and it quickly became one of Copland's best-known and most-performed concert works. Copland followed it with several more versions, including an orchestration of the full ballet score in 1954 and his 1967 *Variations on a Shaker Melody*. Meanwhile *Appalachian Spring* remained a staple in the repertoire of Graham and her company, not only as a regularly performed stage work but also, in 1958, as a television film, which was released the following year and has been commercially available for decades, first as a videocassette and then as a DVD (with bonus material).

This simple chronology hides a complex question: what exactly is *Appalachian Spring*? A purist might point to the premiere, a dance scholar to Graham's choreography, a musicologist to Copland's score(s), and a cultural historian to its manifold incarnations and adaptations over time. *Appalachian Spring* provides a fascinating case study with which to reflect on the nature of an artwork, especially within so collaborative a medium as modern dance. Moreover, the music of at least one version of *Appalachian Spring* assumed a life independent of the choreography and staging, perhaps even overshadowing it. At the heart of the question lies the so-called work concept, encapsulated in an ideal form that, in Western art music, has historically been associated with the score. In this aesthetic view, a performance is but an imperfect and ephemeral manifestation that only approximates the work to some lesser or greater degree.[1]

But through its complicated history of creation and reception, *Appalachian Spring* challenges the work concept and opens an exciting pathway to thinking about it in new ways. First, however, we need to lay bare the traps into which prior commentaries on the piece have fallen. For example, music scholars—with their typical interest in a work's genesis—have tended to situate and even explain Copland's compositional choices as directly linked to the scenario that Graham provided for the ballet in 1943, before he began work on the score. Her final choreography, and the plot it conveyed, are not taken into account save by way of this scenario, even though—as Copland himself admitted—the end result was very different from what he imagined as he wrote the piece. For their part, dance scholars have focused almost exclusively on Graham's choreography, its relationship to the scenario, its place in Graham's overall oeuvre, and its connection to other modern-dance works. Copland's music is for the most part absent from the discussion or appears just incidentally. Additionally, in modern dance, choreographers are usually considered the intellectual owners of a work. In Graham's case this point has led to an acrimonious and protracted legal battle between her heir, Ron Protas, and the Martha Graham Dance Company over the ownership of her works and the rights thereto. Finally, Copland's arrangement of *Appalachian Spring* as a suite, divorced from the dancing, has produced numerous analyses that treat it as a folk-inspired concert work. Rare are such enterprises as Marta Robertson's attempt to explore the integration of music and choreography through her rhythmic analysis of both dance and score. But the question remains: what are we talking about when we speak of *Appalachian Spring*?[2]

For the music, matters are not helped by the fact that while the 1945 orchestral suite is easily available, the original 1944 score for thirteen instruments—three woodwinds (flute, clarinet, and bassoon), piano, double string quartet

   AARON COPLAND'S *APPALACHIAN SPRING*

(two each of violin I, violin II, viola, and cello), and double bass—is not, save by way of renting it from Copland's publisher, Boosey & Hawkes, or by consulting his original manuscript at the Library of Congress. The complete score is also rarely performed outside the ballet, although there is a useful 1994 recording by the Saint Paul Chamber Orchestra. For the dance, the issue is rendered still more complex by Graham's extensive revision of the choreography between the Washington premiere and the New York performance six months later, and by her continuing to rework it over the succeeding years for different dancers with their distinct abilities. This makes the 1958 film a document of one particular historical moment in the performance history of the work, but not a reconstruction of the 1944 (Washington) or 1945 (New York) performances. Indeed, if one compares the 1958 film to the surviving footage of a silent 16-millimeter film from the time of the premiere, both the choreography and the style of dancing reveal significant differences, especially for the roles of the Pioneer Woman and the Bride. Ethel Winter, a dancer with the Graham Company between 1944 and 1969, commented in a 2007 interview on the changes in Graham's performance of the Bride: "When Martha did that role for the movie, I really did wish that it had been done five or ten years earlier because I remember her giving some spectacular performances." As other dancers interviewed for the DVD release of the 1958 film pointed out, the original editor did not properly coordinate movement and music in several passages, leaving them out of sync in ways that were "terribly sad."[3]

The first audiences for *Appalachian Spring* found in their programs the following note:

> Part and parcel of our lives is that moment of Pennsylvania spring when there was "a garden eastward in Eden."
>
> Spring was celebrated by a man and a woman building a house with joy and love and prayer; by a revivalist and his followers in their shouts of exaltation; by a pioneering woman with her dreams of a Promised Land.

Replete with biblical echoes of the Garden of Eden (the note quotes Genesis 2:8) and the Promised Land, it evoked an idealized frontier life, where faith means joy, love, and exaltation, and where pioneering feats can lead to dreams of a glorious future. It set the audience's expectations up for a "shining and joyous number" (as the fashionable *Mayfair* magazine described the work), one that was seen as celebrating the youth of the nation and anticipating postwar prosperity. *Appalachian Spring* was the final piece on the Washington program, ending the evening on a high note.[4]

Music, dance, and stage set merged into a spellbinding performance that held the audience at the edge of their seats. Graham had received from Copland a score that was at the same time tightly constructed and episodic, echoing the narrative features of her 1943 script. She integrated the score's character into her choreography not only by matching obvious formal sections and kinetic elements in music and dance, but also through more subtle correspondences, both structural and stylistic. Yet the dance—despite compressing and transforming elements of the script—changed the dramatic arch into a plot that, at times, stands crosswise (especially in the second part) to the music. Furthermore, just as Noguchi and Copland had drawn on a range of intertexts, so did Graham in her choreography. Perhaps the most striking aspect of *Appalachian Spring* is her play on other stage genres: the integration of ballet movements into her modern-dance style as well as the use of operatic tropes as a narrative device by freezing the action of the dancers onstage during individual solos and duets, as if these were arias in an opera (Figure 3.2).

FIGURE 3.2   Erick Hawkins as the Husbandman with the cast for the first production of *Appalachian Spring*, Library of Congress, Coolidge Auditorium, October 1944, photographer unknown. Library of Congress, Music Division, Elizabeth Sprague Coolidge Collection.

Pearl Lang, who—after years dancing as one of the Followers—took on the role of the Bride, made this point explicitly when she commented that "*Appalachian Spring* is choreographed almost like an opera—the soloists all have arias." This tableau-like quality of the choreography invites the audience members to focus on the individual numbers, anchoring them, however fleetingly, in the moment.[5]

The performance that unfolded on the stage then—as it does now—was an ensemble piece with four powerful figures (and dancers). About the 1945 New York production, the critic Edwin Denby noted the "striking novelty" that the work was "no passionate monodrama of subjective experience but an objective conflict united in its theme," where "each character dominated the stage equally." What might have contributed to Denby's characterization of the work as "objective" was the constant shift of perspective achieved by the chain of relatively short segments that cut cinematographically from one character to another. This choreographic strategy works in sync with the episodic nature of the music, lending the work a prismatic quality that is hard to capture by parsing the score according to the larger segments in Copland's concert suite. The following overview of the music and dance is deliberately fragmented to resist such parsing and instead shows the work's fast-changing pace. Given that the 1958 film is the version easiest accessed by readers today, the following discussion is cued to the film's timings as it is reproduced on *Martha Graham: Dance on Film* (Criterion DVD, 2007). Likewise, my account of the choreography is based (unless otherwise mentioned) on this iteration of the work, though, as noted above, it has differences from the original 1944 version, and also from later ones authorized by Martha Graham and her successors.[6]

APPALACHIAN SPRING *ONSTAGE*

The stage was bathed in bright light, carefully calibrated by the lighting designer Jean Rosenthal to evoke a sunny spring day—a decision that drew positive comments from reviewers at the time. Isamu Noguchi's sparse set (designed to be portable for subsequent productions) framed the space with strong diagonals that added perspective and depth despite the small stage of the Coolidge Auditorium (see again Figure 2.2). The first performance used not only the well-known house set, a diagonal prop playing on a pulpit, and a fence, but also two triangular flats in front—creating a modernist proscenium—and three angled drops. They show Noguchi's sculptural conception of the space and further reflect the hybridity Noguchi sought between Japanese and Western art (see chapter 2). Moreover, the marked diagonals and the short segment of fence referred simultaneously to Noguchi's earlier stage set for Graham in *Frontier* (1935) and to recent productions with similar settings, such as Oliver Smith's drop for *Rodeo* (1942) and the set by Lemuel Ayers for *Oklahoma!* (1943). Edythe Gilford, costume designer for the Graham Company, had created outfits similarly reminiscent of these recent productions while also using colors to group the dancers (see Figure 3.3). Graham wore a dress in cream-colored taffeta with thin, light green stripes, Hawkins a light shirt, and both sported small, dark ties and had their heads

FIGURE 3.3   Set and cast for the first production of *Appalachian Spring*,
Library of Congress, Coolidge Auditorium, October 1944,
photographer unknown. Library of Congress, Music Division,
Elizabeth Sprague Coolidge Collection.

uncovered. The Revivalist (in dark brown) and the Pioneer
Woman (in a warm brown) formed a second visual pair. The
four Followers, dressed in light blue, added a touch of color
to what was otherwise a fairly monochromatic production,
rendered even more so in modern perception through the
black-and-white photography and films.[7]

Copland's music also mixes light and shade. It begins
softly, as the curtain rises on an empty stage. While at first
we hear a simple A major triad outlined in the clarinet, the
next moment brings the unfolding of two superimposed
chords in flute, violin, and viola, with the tonic held as a
pedal in the cello (Example 3.1). This famous polychord

    AARON COPLAND'S *APPALACHIAN SPRING*

stacks an E major triad in second inversion (the dominant chord) on top of an A major triad in first inversion
(Example 3.2). The instrumentation creates a fascinating
timbral play between the flute that laces these six notes into
an ascending line and the strings underscoring the arpeggiated chord with a sustained one that expands as each
note is added. Almost like a period at the end of a sen-
tence, measure 7 brings another iteration of the pedal A,
this time with the piano added an octave below, completing
what—in its sparsity—is a highly modernist sound world,
if one rooted in long-standing (some would say, timeless)

elements of tonal music and using topoi such as the drone of the musette or the shepherd's flute, both symbolizing the pastoral. This opening polychord becomes the foundation on which much of *Appalachian Spring* is built, not only in terms of harmony but also, more important, insofar as the work's melodic lines, tonalities, and timbres are concerned. But those highly condensed first six measures of *Appalachian Spring* also define musical space by way of a no less economical palette than Noguchi's set in physical terms: they share the same traditional-modernist inflections, mixing iconic Americana with more cosmopolitan overtones. Copland later mused about the unique quality of this opening, dubbing it "strangely satisfying in itself" but also expressing surprise "that such a thing hadn't been used in that manner before (at least I don't know of its having been) because it seems almost obvious."[8]

EXAMPLE 3.2   Polychord over A, derived from mm. 4–6.

VERY SLOWLY: FULL ENSEMBLE (0:45)

Into the visual and sonic space created by Noguchi and Copland walk slowly, one by one, the characters of *Appalachian Spring*: in 1944, it was first the Revivalist (Merce Cunningham) with his four female Followers (Nina Fonaroff, Pearl Lang, Marjorie Mazia, and Yuriko),

AARON COPLAND'S *APPALACHIAN SPRING*

then the Pioneer Woman (May O'Donnell), and finally the Husbandman (Erick Hawkins) and Bride (Martha Graham), though in 1958 the sequence is changed. The music is harmonically static in a bright A major sonority, its texture shimmering through the elasticity achieved by the subtle metrical shifts of the repeatedly unfolding polychord; just as the characters are introduced, so are the various instruments and their sonic configurations. In addition to the tonic and dominant triads presented simultaneously (in the polychord) and successively, the subdominant (D major) finds its place, completing the three primary chords of the key. Copland's evocation—but not literal following—of traditional harmony indicates a sound world of the past in ways similar to the modernist reinterpretation of folk dance and Prairie School architecture in the choreography and stage set. But melodies also start to take shape by way of a lyrical motive in the upper register of the violin that juxtaposes a lower neighbor-note motion and then a falling fourth and fifth spanning an octave. With their measured entrance, the characters take ownership of the performance space from the house to the pulpit to the fence.[9]

ALLEGRO: PIONEER WOMAN AND FOLLOWERS (2:33)

A lively Allegro sets the action in motion, with a "dialogue" between the Pioneer Woman and the four Followers. In gestures that draw on folk dance as well as a balletic *pas de quatre*, the four Followers move in counterpoint to the Pioneer Woman in a segment that merges everyday concerns with morning prayers. The score begins with a lively new idea, played vigorously in piano and strings, followed by the polychord running almost humorously in staccato through the bassoon and clarinet. The second theme, played against the first, is more of a chorale (for the prayers). This is the melody Copland had developed in Hollywood (see again Example 2.1) while working on *The North Star*, but it finds its place in *Appalachian Spring* by Copland's using a version of its first three notes in the introduction. His play with multiple motives also leads to the inventive rhythmic layering that was an important part of Copland's sonic texture: while the polychord unfolds in the upper voices stressing the second beat, the melodic line in the bass emphasizes the first and third. Then the slow and not entirely regular rhythm of the chorale-like melody adds another kinetic dimension to which the piano contributes fast eighth notes—only to dissolve into the concluding arpeggiated polychords. Their lighthearted staccato movement is picked up—in a witty contrast to their upward motion—by the Followers as they take their seats on the bench.

MODERATO: HUSBANDMAN (5:25)

The Husbandman's brief solo reveals a confident young man, commanding the space of the stage and blending folk-dance jumps and thigh slapping with balletic pirouettes, expressive gestures, and a show of athletic prowess. As with the handclapping of the Followers in the prior Allegro, his thigh slapping is carefully synchronized with the music, which Copland distills into the rhythmic accompaniment of an absent dance melody, interspersed with the portions

   AARON COPLAND'S *APPALACHIAN SPRING*

of the chorale from the previous section. Copland will use this chorale extract as punctuation in a number of subsequent segments (Example 3.3).[10]

EXAMPLE 3.3   Aaron Copland, *Appalachian Spring*, rehearsal score, rehearsal number 18, *ACC*, box 76.

MUCH SLOWER: HUSBANDMAN AND BRIDE (6:36)

The lyrical duet of Husbandman and Bride introduces a new theme, though it is closely linked motivically to the previous segment, overlapping through the final two measures with a descending melodic line (in a woodwind sonority)—later coupled with the chorale extract—that then punctuates the duet's three sections, made up of parallel strophes. This creates yet another close motivic connection between the various episodes that contributes to the taut construction of the score which Graham found so appealing, while allowing Copland to shift character kaleidoscopically from one segment to the next. Graham's choreography keeps the Husbandman and Bride in close contact and often in parallel motion, while the ending allows for a more widely spaced dialogue with complementary gestures before joining the couple together in a walk back to the house.

A lighthearted fast section in the style of a square dance accompanies the Revivalist and his flock. Starting out in B major, it takes on a very different character from the earlier Allegro shared by the Pioneer Woman and the four Followers. This is Copland in his most *Rodeo*-like vein, perhaps because he originally designed this segment for the wedding celebrations in Graham's scenario. The actual choreography becomes a dance oscillating between religious fervor (channeled through the Revivalist's prayers) and playful courting that reveals enough sexual undertones as the music increases in intensity to lead the Pioneer Woman to intercede before things get out of hand. Both in the 1958 film and in Cunningham's earlier rendering of the role, the Revivalist is clearly portrayed as a young preacher, seduced just as easily as he incites passion—religious and otherwise—in his followers. The Pioneer Woman, by contrast, serves as ultimate authority, a matriarch who has seen it all and who knows when to step in and when to let things play out.

MOLTO MODERATO: PIONEER WOMAN AND FOLLOWERS (11:16)

Reaching E major, the Molto moderato section, though short, is weighty, thanks to its grandiose dotted rhythms and majestic homophonic chords. The melody transforms the violin motive from the introduction, with its lower neighbor-note motion, then the falling fourth and fifth (but now a fifth and fourth). The section plays out the Pioneer Woman's intercession by turning the Followers and the Revivalist back into their respective proper positions on the pulpit and the church bench before moving into a brief solo prayer, the punctuating chorale extract now acting as a period.

ALLEGRO–PRESTO: BRIDE (12:21)

The Bride's solo starts with a fast section that echoes the rhythmic and motivic elements of the Husbandman's solo (the Moderato, above), a sonic correspondence reinforced by the instrumentation, which separates out the patterns of the melody and accompaniment across discrete combinations (woodwinds, strings, and piano). The Allegro seems to hiccup its way into action as Copland keeps the meter shifting and constantly pauses the movement, only to start up again. The Presto, in a clear C major presented as if parenthetically, immediately establishes a consistent kinetic energy driven by repeated eighth notes. It is remarkable what Copland can do with simple ascending and descending scales, with the apparent references to Stravinsky's *Petroushka* (1911) and *Symphony in C* (1940; note the key) adding playful intertextuality. Graham's subdued dance style in the 1958 film (when she was sixty-four years old) clashes somewhat with the music's exuberance. Reports from the early performance speak of her solo as "a dance of joy, a joy so big she cannot contain it. She whirls and runs and blows phantom kisses." John Martin describes Graham as melding "such a radiant quality of the vision of youth into a longed-for and, indeed, predestined fulfillment that she is likely to bring tears very close to the surface of more than one pair of eyes. Nowhere in her entire repertoire is there a more enchanting passage."[11]

This is a short transition that, in the score, serves as a coda to the Presto, but Graham uses its statement of the chorale (now in a fuller version, and varied to end with lush A major sonorities) to create another "duet" between the Revivalist and his flock before the full cast processes slowly across the stage. The segment ends with a firm, deliberately "manly" handshake between Husbandman and Revivalist, and a gentle embrace of the Pioneer Woman and the Bride.

At the center of the work is this short ensemble piece, one whose choreography might represent a wedding, a blessing, or even a "Sunday Walk," as Graham noted on the rehearsal score (one of the very few notes in her hand); some vestiges of the last remain when the four main characters head off for a leisurely stroll after the Revivalist's blessing of the couple. The music here is, in effect, a reprise of Copland's introduction to the ballet, but now a semitone lower, evoking A-flat major. This segment transitions into perhaps the best-known portion of *Appalachian Spring*, the theme and variations on "Simple Gifts," also beginning in A-flat major and plainly inhabiting the harmonic space of traditional tonality associated with such tunes. Copland introduces the melody by way of a slower statement in two-part canon in the strings (this is omitted in the Suite). He considered this a "Transition" (as he marked it in the piano score), although Graham choreographed it as the beginning of her dance between Husbandman and Bride while the other character retake their "frozen" positions at 17:36.

THEME AND VARIATIONS: BRIDE AND HUSBANDMAN (17:49)

Over Copland's theme and four variations, Graham choreographed a rondo that intersperses short moments of pair dancing with longer alternating solos, two for the Bride and two for the Husbandman, starting her first solo on the theme itself. The dance style of both characters plays on folk dances, such as, for example, in the lovely reference to an Irish jig in the Bride's second solo, but the choreography also draws on more balletic *pas de deux* traditions. Ending the couple's duet with the cadence of the fourth variation, Graham gave the concluding statement of the theme—at half speed and this time in canon between clarinet and flute—to the four Followers as they prepare the Revivalist for his solo.

RATHER SLOW–FAST: REVIVALIST (20:33)

Copland's score changes register abruptly toward a bleaker sonority in response to Graham's original prompt: the arrival of a fugitive slave. It presents a markedly modernist soundscape, all the more jarring in its sharp contrast with the harmonic language of the variations. This section is a dark mirror of the Pioneer Woman's Allegro (at 2:33), and one where Copland's score becomes the most filmic in terms of its use of disconnected gestures, "hurry" music, and isolated "stingers." It is also the most fragmented part of *Appalachian Spring*. Graham turned it into the

Revivalist's dance, offering a fascinating view on how she and Cunningham envisaged representing an ecstatically possessed preacher from Appalachia, from the opening genuflection to the shaking limbs and wild jumps. Critics of the time had a field day writing about this "volcanic dance of exhortation" with its "wild leaps and bounds." The "fire and brimstone in the preacher's voodoo-like dance" was described as "the most gripping moment in the ballet," a solo "mounting in a fury of jungle-born rhythms. Music and dance joined in stunning power here." Edwin Denby saw the Revivalist as a composite of Saint Francis and Thoreau, merging "evangelism with animism." All three critics cited here draw on a linguistic register that is coded as describing African American dance, a connotation that might have been in the choreographer's mind—given the music's original association with the fugitive slave—but one that moves the Revivalist even further away from the New England Puritanism routinely associated with this role.[12]

VERY DELIBERATE: PIONEER WOMAN AND HUSBANDMAN (22:00)

As before, it is the Pioneer Woman who intercedes. Her prayer leads into a brief and tender—almost consoling— duet with the Husbandman, which is followed by his second solo, one that seems to use gestures of rural life (including a set of lasso-roping movements that might be read as a humorous wink at de Mille's choreographies for *Rodeo* and *Oklahoma!*) almost as an antidote to the Revivalist's passionate sermon and prayer. The music, however, appears designed for something else—or, perhaps better, for nothing at all, given that Copland seems to be riffing rather aimlessly on the arpeggiated polychord of the opening, an impression strengthened by an elusive displacement of the beat. Copland's score here gives an almost neutral sonic space for Graham to fill with its own brief episode.

TWICE AS FAST: REVIVALIST AND FOLLOWERS (24:08)

This time the Revivalist and his Followers remain undisturbed in their dance to a short, fast piece that brings the music from their first dance (Fast) back in a distorted A major (over B minor harmony) and then evoking D-flat major, subverting the earlier segment's more functional harmonic language. The dance ends with the Revivalist lying backward on top of, and surrounded by, the four Followers.

MOLTO ALLEGRO ED AGITATO: BRIDE (25:27)

Just as the Revivalist and the Followers have music that reconfigures that of their first dance, so does the music that Graham choreographed as the Bride's second solo echo the kinetic drive of her first one, even though motivically there is little connection. Harmonically speaking. it is the least stable part of the entire work, in clear contrast to its earlier evocations of common-practice tonality. Choreographically, this is a darker dance veering between devotion and doubt, with movements that are tighter and lower than in the Bride's first solo and that, especially in the 1944 version, abandoned any earlier gestures that might allude to folk dance for panicky, jerky movements traversing the space both indoors and outdoors until, having worked through her fears—whether of frontier life or of marriage and motherhood remains open—the Bride settles on the rocking chair.

The final scene combines the last six measures of Copland's previous section, marked Meno mosso and presenting the chorale in the form it was heard at the end of the Bride's first solo, with the last part of the score. Graham designed the short, lyrical passage in C major as a brief duet between Bride and Husbandman. Then, from underneath the lyrical theme, the Shaker melody emerges as the Followers and Revivalist join the dance of Husbandman and Bride. As the final, augmented statement of "Simple Gifts" is played "Broadly" and fortissimo, the Pioneer Woman takes the Revivalist's place, once more dancing with the Followers. But this affirmative apotheosis of the theme is not the end of the work. Instead, Copland moves to a hymnlike passage, marked pianissimo and *misterioso*. This is entirely new material—for all that one might find traces of its melodic and harmonic elements earlier in the score—yet it belongs wholly to, and even seems to define, the *Appalachian Spring* sound world. We then (at the Andante) have a final reprise of the familiar chorale, first heard combined with the energetic Allegro theme for the Pioneer Woman and Followers, though now it stands peacefully alone, and in a more complete form than when it was used just for punctuation. The palindromic structure outlined following the variations of "Simple Gifts," reprising prior material in reverse order, reaches its logical conclusion in the final measures, which return to the opening, with its motion through the tonic triad (now on C) and fading out on a long, sustained version of the polychord. But the palindrome does not so much bring things back to the beginning as emphasize their continuation through the seasonal cycles of life. Here, too, the choreography tells a related story: the characters leave the stage in single file, but Husbandman and Bride remain as if posing for an old-fashioned family photograph, frozen in time but for all time (see later, Figure 4.1). It is a subtle reference to Grant Wood's *American Gothic* (1930), though one replacing the grim stoicism of the Depression with a more optimistic vision for a postwar America.

APPALACHIAN SPRING *IN CONCERT*

By the time he composed *Appalachian Spring*, Copland had perfected the art of adapting his dance and film scores for the concert hall. *Rodeo* had proven a major success with orchestras across the United States, and *Appalachian Spring* would as well. But the dance score, as Copland pointed out, was too fragmented and disparate in character to work on its own. Both the program of the suite's premiere and the published orchestral score carry a short notice that gives the composition's background and explains that it is "a condensed version of the ballet, retaining all essential features but omitting those sections in which the interest is primarily choreographic." In addition, the orchestration was changed to a full symphony orchestra, including a large contingent of percussion instruments, from snare drum to xylophone.[13]

Copland completely excised the darker, eight-minute portion between the end of the theme and variations and the tune's magnified restatement (marked "Broadly"). He also cut smaller sections throughout the dance score and condensed certain passages, for example by eliminating motivic repetitions. The biggest intervention with the remaining material occurred in the theme and variations. Copland took out the initial canonic statement of the theme in viola and violin (the "Transition" noted above), so that its first presentation stood out far more noticeably, also allowing him to save the canonic possibilities for later. He then reordered the variation set by cutting Variation 2 and replacing it with Variation 4, and he composed a new, contrapuntal one (now Variation 4 of the suite) and revised Variation 3 significantly. The new sequence offers clearer differences between the variations, especially by setting the contrapuntal texture of the new Variation 4 in contrast to the massed homophonic chords of the tune's final statement in what is now Variation 5.[14]

The episodic character of the dance score for *Appalachian Spring* required a stronger compositional intervention in this reworking for the concert stage than the more cohesive five-movement score for Agnes de Mille's *Rodeo*, where the excision of the original fourth episode was sufficient to configure the music into a quasi-symphonic four-movement structure. Yet despite Copland's more substantial revisions in the case of *Appalachian Spring*, the suite kept its character as a kaleidoscopic set of dances, perhaps reflecting a deliberate decision by the composer to reference the baroque dance suite (and its neoclassical recasting by composers from Ravel to Milhaud) rather than the symphony.

Whereas in 1942 a symphonic *Rodeo* suite fit the needs of an American concert life keen on displaying artistic credibility, in October 1945 a victorious nation could allow for a more lighthearted, transnational play on neoclassical concert music, including an even more marked evocation of Stravinsky by emphasizing the references to his music in the expanded, sparkling orchestration. Moreover, Copland was already hard at work on a symphony proper—indeed, he finished its slow movement while at work on the *Appalachian Spring* suite—and his Third Symphony would be premiered the following year, in 1946.[15]

The concert suite has created a conundrum for listeners and performers, for it changed the character of the piece rather drastically. By cutting the darker, more dissonant section between Variation 4 and the final restatement of the Shaker hymn, Copland had now fashioned a piece of joyful and unruffled Americana, perfectly suited to a triumphant postwar United States advertising the nation's virtues both at home and to the world at large. It is in that sanitized guise that *Appalachian Spring* was recorded and broadcast for decades, and it is the version most listeners have come to love. One reviewer on Amazon's website even reported that he was so annoyed by the unfamiliar music of the complete ballet score in the 1999 recording by the San Francisco Symphony Orchestra that he created a listening version which cut out the offending section. Even professional musicians can be startled: more than one player hired by the Martha Graham Dance Company asked the music director whether they had added the music to Copland's score for the purpose of the choreography. Such reactions are more than amusing anecdotes.

They are at the heart of the question with which the chapter began—what is *Appalachian Spring*?—and they are closely connected to how audiences responded to and engaged with this work in its many versions, both at the time of its creation during World War II and in the seven decades since.[16]

CHAPTER 4

AMERICANA BETWEEN WAR AND PEACE

Everyone says *Appalachian Spring* is glorious.
How I long to hear it.
> *Pfc. Lincoln Kirstein (a "Monuments Man"), letter from*
> *Germany to Aaron Copland, June 16, 1945*

WORLD WAR II AND its aftermath punctuated the early history of *Appalachian Spring*. The work's two-year gestation between the commission in 1942 and the premiere in 1944 spanned the most intense years of the war, and Martha Graham and Aaron Copland responded accordingly. Not only did Graham's scenario outline a Civil War drama as a mirror of contemporary concerns, but Copland's score also reflected many of the war-related details of her narrative, from the agitated evocation of a fugitive slave's fearful escape to the dissonant-rich "Day of Wrath" episode that Graham had described as having "the qualities of the Harper's Ferry incident." Graham's 1944 choreography, however, recast the plot as a spring celebration at the American frontier. Copland's music remained unchanged at this point, causing some problems in matching it with the new narrative, as, for instance, in the Bride's second solo. Yet he too responded to the political shifts when he created his concert suite as the war ended in Europe and then (by the time of its premiere by the New York Philharmonic Orchestra) in the Pacific, and as the United States was busy building a postwar world under the covenant of the Pax Americana.[1]

Although the creation of *Appalachian Spring* straddled war and peace, its reception was shaped by a public discourse that—despite ongoing military action—had already turned toward postwar life in America. Having fought for freedom and democracy abroad, the nation now faced the problems of reintegrating millions of veterans, of reconfiguring civil life after women and minorities had moved into jobs traditionally held by white males, and of establishing its new position as a world leader on the political and economic stage. Consequently, audiences and critics responded most strongly to those markers of national identity in *Appalachian Spring* that corresponded to this postwar-oriented public discourse. No one seemed even to have registered the darker sonorities of the score inspired by conflict-related episodes in Graham's "House of Victory" scenario, instead hearing the music of *Appalachian Spring* only as a bright, folk-inspired piece of happy Americana. Through this lens of unmitigated national optimism, reviewers focused in particular on four issues: the construction of spring and youthfulness as symbols for American vitality, the frontier as a foundational myth of the United States, the location of national and regional identities, and the positive aspects of artistic and social conventionality.

An article in *Time* magazine in May 1945 quoted Martha Graham's claim that *Appalachian Spring* was "purely symbolic of the springtime of the nation." Whether or not those were her exact words, the association of her choreography with spring and youthful nationhood had by that time become staple fixtures in critical responses to it. Her program note had already connected the construction of a house with the season of spring and therefore implied the symbolism of nation building. Reviewers then carried this association in two directions, both intimately linked to broader rhetorical gambits of the time: they tied the spring of the nation to its pioneer days, casting the modern United States as now somehow more mature and therefore fit for international leadership; and at the same time, youthfulness was presented as an essential and timeless character trait of the American identity.[2]

George Beiswanger, for instance, treated *Appalachian Spring* as a period piece, one that represented an earlier time of "spring in the history of our country." Miles Kastendieck also declared it "symbolic of the Spring of young America looking toward new frontiers with an ecstasy of high hopes," while Robert A. Hague continued the theme of locating the work firmly in the nation's past as "one of those frontier pieces which attempts to express the pioneer spirit of young America." The setup of characters was perfect for this reading, for Graham's choreography presented a number of archetypal figures: a youthful couple contributing to the new nation with their homesteading, and a wise older woman as a source of embodied wisdom. Indeed, neither the Pioneer Woman in *Appalachian Spring* nor Aunt Eller in *Oklahoma!* (one of the intertexts for Graham's choreography) was unique in that respect: both were part of the nation's founding mythologies.[3]

Several other critics, however, drew on a different, more essentialist understanding of America (and Americans) as eternally young and intrepid. For the reviewer in *Dance* magazine, the youthfulness pervading *Appalachian Spring* equated "American daring." More poignant, however, is the review that the German Jewish dance critic Artur Michel published in *Aufbau*, an anti-fascist German-language weekly with a circulation of forty thousand among the Jewish exile community in the United States. The title of his review rechristened *Appalachian Spring* as "American Spring" (*Amerikanischer Frühling*): its youthful looking forward, not back, made it American in its very essence (*ein urameri-kanisches Werk*), and to watch Graham dance the role of the Bride was "to witness the emergence of the future."[4]

What Michel claimed encapsulated a timeless American essence—youthfulness and the active pursuit of a greater future—were highly contested concepts during World War II. The youth cult of Nazi Germany and Adolf Hitler's proclamation of the current present as the dawn of a thousand-year empire were countered in the United States with the argument that true youthfulness was essentially American and that the future of the world lay in the path of American exceptionalism, with its frontier spirit and belief in individual achievement. Michel's explicitly anti-fascist reading of *Appalachian Spring* as the artistic embodiment of an essentially timeless American Spring thus located the future very markedly on this side of the Atlantic. He saw it as a highly political work not because it dealt with the pioneer days of yesteryear—Michel barely alludes to the setting—but because it transcended historical specificity in stating a universal truth: *Appalachian Spring* was authentic less to a time and place than to the spirit of the nation.

FRONTIER FANTASIES

Appalachian Spring reflects a change in the way in which the American frontier was imagined during World War II. Gone was the prairie nationalism of *Rodeo*, with its deliberate emphasis on lasso-roping cowboys tackling whatever obstacle life in the West threw at them. Instead, the work harked back to the frontier as a Garden of Eden, a Promised Land imagined as a pristine space within which to celebrate the building of a nation in the spirit of renewal (rather than conquest). Graham's frontier was one defined by its pioneer character, but it was also a space of community building at its most elemental. This was not a frontier in need of masculinist conquest, but one that nourished "the fine and simple idealism" that, explained the dance critic John Martin, animates "the highest human motives." Stepping away from the overtly expansionist frontier myth of earlier prairie nationalism, *Appalachian Spring* offered an alternative and more peaceful vision of the frontier that contrasted with the expansionist politics of the Axis powers.[5]

Martha Graham was well aware of the issues. She kept among her papers a transcript of a Nazi propaganda radio broadcast from June 1941, in English and addressed directly to her, by Max Otto Koischwitz, who had taught in the German departments of Columbia and Hunter College in the 1930s before returning in 1939 to Berlin, where he became a leading propaganda warrior at German State Radio. Koischwitz made it clear that political frontiers in Europe were soon to change in favor of Germany. He continued by evoking his memories of seeing Graham's 1935 ballet *Frontier*: "But your Frontier, Martha Graham, will remain unchanged and unaffected by political and social evolutions because your Frontier is not a political borderline, it is the eternal frontier between home and world outside. The borderline between security and adventure; between the known and the unknown." This comment was all the more inflammatory because just before this, Koischwitz in his broadcast had contrasted the masculinity of German culture with the effeminacy of America, symbolized by Graham herself: "Strange as it may seem, whenever I think of American, of specifically American art, I cannot help thinking of your art, Martha Graham. Is it perhaps because the United States depends far more on women than on men? The American boy is dominated by his mother; the American husband by his wife and the American father by his daughter. If one thinks of specifically German art, one would never think of a woman." Graham's frontier, then, was cast as domestic, feminized, and politically impotent.[6]

It is hard to say how much of this was in her mind eighteen months later when she developed the "House of Victory" scenario, and yet—with its emphasis on the Civil War, *Uncle Tom's Cabin*, and John Brown—that scenario seems written to counter the feminized and depoliticized vision of the American frontier that Koischwitz had attributed to her. Even though she reworked and condensed these particulars in her 1944 choreography, *Appalachian Spring* did present a frontier that was following a more masculine-dominated gender order, especially where her own role as the Bride was concerned.

It would have been easy to regender the frontier, but unlike earlier "American" ballets by Lincoln Kirstein and Agnes de Mille, there are no outlaws or cowboys in *Appalachian Spring*. Rather, Graham performed the neat trick of treating her new frontier as a bigendered space where women and men alike had essential roles—distinct, perhaps, but certainly complementary. More than one critic read the final pose of the Bride and Husbandman (Figure 4.1) as a vision of a new democracy: according to the dance critic Robert Sabin, the Bride (Graham) sat on the rocking

FIGURE 4.1   Martha Graham (Bride) and Erick Hawkins (Husbandman) at
the first production of *Appalachian Spring*, Library of Congress,
Coolidge Auditorium, October 1944, photographer unknown.
Library of Congress, Music Division, Elizabeth Sprague Coolidge
Collection.

chair "as upon a throne with her husband standing at her side, a moment of quiet majesty which is unforgettable. Here is democracy in action, a vision like Whitman's, of simple people with the dignity of kings." Likewise, Claudia Cassidy, writing for the *Chicago Tribune* in 1946, thought that "at the close, when husband and wife take possession of their dwelling, there is a gentle yet royal dignity about the gesture. This man's house is his castle, his wife is its queen."[7]

The notion of rural Americans displaying "royal dignity," or Sabin's "dignity of kings," might seem odd in the context of U.S. history, but it is far less so when treated as an abstraction within the rhetoric of American exceptionalism and its biblical overtones. Abstraction figured prominently in *Appalachian Spring* in other ways, too, not least in the choreography's allusions to folk dance and Noguchi's skeleton set. This was a far cry from the rural realism of the likes of Grant Wood and Thomas Hart Benton (famous as a regionalist painter and muralist) in the previous decade. But again, critics were well able to read the codes, granting the abstract referents a far more universal significance. For the set, Margaret Lloyd knew very well what was being represented: "a small house in the wilderness, with front steps and a single rocking-chair to make it home," plus a "side porch bench that in due course serves for a semblance of church service, and a fence." It is her reading of the fence, however, that is most striking: "a fence that indicates pastures and woodlands—all America—beyond." It develops a powerful trope: here is an idealized frontier, a bucolic landscape where even the snake that created havoc in Eden was now tamed by full-blooded pioneers.[8]

Where reviewers located this pastoral frontier and how they interpreted it were closely intertwined with other discursive interventions during the construction of the postwar nation. In this respect, and despite Graham's and Copland's progressive politics, *Appalachian Spring* contributed its share to the forging of a brave new world of homogenized middle-class America, one that was white and Protestant. Graham had already created geographical ambiguity by combining her title's reference to the Southern mountain region of Appalachia with a program note that located the plot in Pennsylvania. Even though the Appalachian Regional Commission includes most of Western Pennsylvania— where Graham grew up—New York reviewers normally located it south of the Mason-Dixon line. Copland's score, with its variations on "Simple Gifts," added another geographical as well as cultural referent, one denoting a sect with communities ranging from Maine to Kentucky, though not, oddly enough, in Appalachia itself (the Shakers were mostly in New England and the Midwest down into Kentucky). While the Shaker connection would dominate the later reception of the work, critics barely mentioned it at first. Instead, they referred to Pennsylvania and Appalachia as if they were the single home of American pioneer prowess, a conflation that was perhaps more political than incompetent because it reconfigured the poor white mountain folks of the Appalachian revival during the 1920s and '30s into somewhat more palatable "ancestors," in the guise of heartland homesteaders, for a nation transforming itself into a global superpower. Edwin Denby made it explicit when he wrote that *Appalachian Spring* was "no glorification by condescending city folk of our rude and simple past" but instead offered "a credible and astonishing evocation of that real time and place," though he was vague as to what that "real" time and place might be.[9]

City folk—to use Denby's term for East Coast urbanites—were, of course, the principal audiences for folk music shows, folk art exhibitions, and Broadway plays based on the evocation of rural America. This hinterland was, however, malleable depending on the needs of the cultural and financial elite. It was also contested ground for various agendas, whether to create an unspoiled counterworld to the industrialized East and Midwest through national parks and other wilderness preserves, or to use folk art to define a wholesome national culture embodying the democratic values of American exceptionalism. By the end of World War II, with a victorious nation that was growing wealthy on the engines of the war industries, the representation of rural America needed to be as far removed as possible from the Great Depression with its dust-bowl poverty and migrant workers. Before Pearl Harbor, a radical modern dancer such as Sophie Maslow could use folk-inspired modern dance to draw attention to poor and battered Oklahoma sharecroppers in her 1941 *Dust Bowl Ballads*, with music by Woody Guthrie (Graham dismissed her dance style as "agricultural"). By the end of the war, a work such as *Appalachian Spring*—or Elie Siegmeister's 1944 romp through American folk music titled *Sing Out, Sweet Land!*—presented a pristine countryside of yesteryear, populated by wholesome, all-American characters—the "shoutin' preacher" included.[10]

To experience Graham's idyllic Appalachia as fully as possible, audiences turned to Copland's music as an enabling soundtrack. Horace Grenell, the music critic for the Communist *Daily Worker*, used the score (rather than Graham's choreography) to fashion Appalachia into a symbol of America proper by declaring, first, that "this music is America," and then commending the composer: "he builds and masses his sounds so that you feel the accumulating bigness of a work that is truly Appalachian." For Kastendieck, on the other hand, it was Graham who presented Appalachia as a stand-in for the nation. "This is no ordinary Spring in the Appalachians," he asserted, but one that was "symbolic of the Spring of young America looking toward new frontiers." Denby, for his part, drew on a familiar trope when he imagined the frontier cabin surrounded by nature, as evoked by the choreography: "The Appalachian isolation of the pioneer farmhouse in the piece is suggested even more imaginatively by a note of wildlife that keeps cropping up in the dances."[11] However, his reading seems to have more in it of Thoreau at Walden Pond than any remote mountain region.

Graham's Appalachia was more northern (Pennsylvania) than southern, with none of the hillbilly associations of moonshine, banjos, and Li'l Abner. Moreover, despite the African American connotations that some of the critics associated rather obliquely with the Revivalist's dance style, and even with the presence of Yuriko among the four Followers, the social world evoked and celebrated in *Appalachian Spring* was white, both ethnically and culturally. Appalachia was presented as uninhabited land, free to be claimed by the pioneers. American Indians did not feature in the choreography—obviously a conscious decision on Graham's part, given that well into 1944 she had thought of the character of an Indian Girl as integral to the plot. Just as the Indian Girl was excised, so was the fugitive slave. Thus *Appalachian Spring* became a work about white America for white audiences, reviewed in the white press for a predominantly white readership. The press lists for the Washington premiere contained no representatives of African American newspapers, and even the New York production received no comment therein (not even the sarcastic aside by W. E. B. Du Bois in the *New York Amsterdam News* that one might expect). So far as the African American press was concerned, *Appalachian Spring* may as well not have existed. Whether the work's 1944–45 audiences were in any way integrated remains an open question. Onstage, however, the "democracy in action" that Sabin evoked so eloquently in his interpretation of the final scene was without question limited to white America.[12]

COMPELLING CONVENTIONALITY

The reactionary aspects of *Appalachian Spring* fit perfectly into its time. Over the four years of American involvement in World War II, artistic production in the United States had taken a turn toward convention. Experimental art did not disappear: the 1944 New York dance recital by Merce Cunningham to compositions by John Cage drew significant local attention, for example. Nonetheless, wartime concerns led to a consolidation of artistic trends that had begun with the Popular Front of the mid-1930s but were now instrumentalized for a socially more conservative agenda. It is no coincidence that *Appalachian Spring* merged a folk-inspired score with a plot dedicated to a celebration of heter-onormative Western society, and with a choreography that drew on more traditional movements from both ballet and folk dance.[13]

Appalachian Spring was not the first modern-dance pro-duction that integrated ballet elements into its choreography; far from it. Nor had ballet resisted the expressive lure of mod-ern dance. In effect, American-themed ballet productions from the late 1930s on, especially those by American Ballet Theatre and Ballet Caravan, used modern-dance movements and featured folk-dance patterns in their choreographies. Two of Copland's scores—for Eugene Loring's *Billy the Kid* (1938) and Agnes de Mille's *Rodeo* (1942)—were written for them. On the other hand, modern-dance choreographers softened the angular and dramatic gestures and contractions of the genre with more regulated ballet patterns. In the case of Martha Graham, however, who had been so vocally and publicly opposed to ballet in the 1930s, the absorption of ballet and folk dance into a modern-dance piece drew significant comment.[14]

Louis Biancolli contrasted the "healthy new trends" of a more "tonic style" and ensembles "geared to rhythms and symmetries that meet standard ballet at least half way" with modern dance's "cubist-like" movements, "especially in sequences featuring the dancer herself." For Biancolli, those more modern sequences made it hard to follow the plot. Other reviewers also referred to the dances for the Bride and Husbandman in terms of ballet: one talked about "a *pas de deux* of sheer tender dance," and another wrote about "ballet lifts with Graham adjustments" that "radiate their happiness." This turn toward a more familiar dance style, and its joyous consequences, also featured in comments on Copland's score, which Sabin thought contained "transparent, really lovely music, as fresh, as lyric and direct as the dancing Miss Graham has conceived." A consensus emerged that *Appalachian Spring* was a popular success because "this newest Graham dance-drama (to Aaron Copland's alternately gay and poignant Pulitzer prize score) was comprehensible even to the bored businessman."[15]

The apparent simplicity and directness of the choreography and score of *Appalachian Spring* served multiple political, social, and cultural agendas as World War II came to a close and the United States prepared for a postwar future. Perhaps inevitably, no critic was yet going to question its rosy vision, nor did any investigate the rather complex path from the "House of Victory" that led there. The same is true of the reception of the orchestral suite, which purged all references to that path. The concert version certainly retained some of the narrative associations of the plot of the final ballet (not least by means of the program note attached to the suite), but in an increasingly generic and idealized form. Thus Warren Storey Smith, the conservative critic for the *Boston Post*, lauded the suite as being "truly American in spirit" because of "its celebration of the emotions of a newly wedded mountain couple about to take possession of their home," focusing far more on the domestic idyll than on any remaining reference to the Pioneer Woman or the Revivalist and Followers. Even the more liberal Rudolph Elie, Jr., of the *Boston Herald*, managed to overcome his shadow of a doubt about the score, although in a rather strange manner: "Maybe I'm naïve or something, but I think the composer really meant what he wrote" when Copland's music evoked "the presentiments of motherhood" or the domestic life of a husband and his wife "so warmly and tenderly." It was an unusual emphasis on the authenticity of a heteronormative and conventional frontier narrative, one that at least opens to readers in the know the possibility that Copland may have donned a musical mask that did not entirely hide the fact that a gay, left-wing, Jewish composer might not entirely have been comfortable with a plot so conventional and conservative as that of *Appalachian Spring*. Yet for the moment, at least, the work's various versions fit well into broader agendas of American society at the end of World War II.[16]

CHAPTER 5

AN AMERICAN ICON

De lindos paisajes, cantos del lugar; montañeses, predicatorio
y luceros.

Carlos Suffern, "Conciertos" (1947)

PIGEONHOLED AS A PIECE of joyful Americana,
Appalachian Spring was eminently suited for a triumphant postwar United States advertising the nation's
positive qualities both at home and to the world at large.
Whether taken on tour by Martha Graham or performed in
its more mobile form in the concert suite, the work became
an important tool of cultural diplomacy. The orchestral version, in particular, quickly made its way across the United
States and even overseas: as the *New York Times* noted,
by May 1946 it had already "been given in Vienna, Sofia,
London, Zurich, and Sydney." In 1948 Leonard Bernstein
conducted it in Italy for his debut concert there. Not only
was *Appalachian Spring* "a wild success" in Milan, as he
reported back to Copland, but one audience member found
that the score reminded him "of American movies." Such

sonic evocation of America and its popular culture would, indeed, be one of the mainstays in the reception of Aaron Copland's score, especially abroad. But the intersections of *Appalachian Spring* with American culture in the twentieth and twenty-first centuries went well beyond its successful performance history. On the one hand, it became tied to the craze for all things Shaker; on the other, its musical idiom became the soundtrack for essentially American qualities, whether in political campaigns or car advertisements. Finally, *Appalachian Spring* turned into a poster child for recent scholarly and artistic trends that have begun to relocate artworks in the contexts of their original creation and to which the present book makes its own contribution. These four issues form the topic of this final chapter.[1]

APPALACHIAN SPRING: AMERICA ABROAD

The United States was comparatively slow in turning to music as a tool for cultural diplomacy. During World War II both the State Department and the newly founded Office of Inter-American Affairs eventually explored how to use music in the pursuit of their twin goals of marketing the American way and of winning the hearts and minds of allies and former enemies. Aaron Copland was fully immersed in this endeavor, serving as a music advisor to both agencies and traveling abroad on their behalf. Dance companies, too, were used in this context, though less frequently than individual musicians because of the exorbitant costs associated with sending an entire ensemble, stage sets and costumes included, on an international tour. When it happened, however, as with Graham's 1955 tour to Asia, it made a big splash. Both Graham and Copland would be important ambassadors for American art during the Cold War, though they began to stand for different aspects of American icon culture.[2]

Appalachian Spring had already been earmarked for potential diplomatic exploitation by the Office of War Information in 1945. It would form the centerpiece of Graham's two State Department–sponsored tours to Asia in 1955 and 1974. While both the State Department and the United States Information Agency (USIA) were keen to present American culture through an all-American choreographer and her modern dance, they also tried to emphasize Graham's cross-cultural credibility by advertising that many of her dance moves were, in effect, inspired by Eastern dance. With Isamu Noguchi's hybrid sets on the one hand, and Copland's folk-inspired score on the other, *Appalachian Spring* fit the bill perfectly. The work was promoted as a "folk tale"—this in India—with local newspapers picking up on its character as "a delightful piece of Americana." Yet press releases and local responses also focused on cultural intersections between Graham's works and Asian art, whether in Noguchi's designs or in her dance movements. Indeed, what distinguished her dance from traditional Western ballet and made it modern was precisely what could be attributed to Eastern influence. Graham's *Appalachian Spring*, then, was the perfect piece for a cultural-diplomacy mission because of its malleability by the performance context. How well this could work is seen in the comment of one Indian reviewer, who considered the pioneer world of *Appalachian Spring* "a much needed corrective to be set against the picture of the fat, well-fed, cigar-smoking American."[3]

By contrast, Copland's music—especially that of *Appalachian Spring*—was associated with more traditional constructions of Americana as folklore-inspired neoclassical concert repertoire, which fared increasingly poorly in the international sphere of the postwar avant-garde. Nonetheless, for official America Copland remained an important cultural export. His music—especially that of the 1940s—was celebrated as a credible form of Americana that traveled well to orchestras across the globe and to which average concertgoers responded with enthusiasm. The problem lay with the same intelligentsia that Graham continued to wow with her choreography and that now considered such scores as *Appalachian Spring* as old-fashioned. The change happened quickly. As early as his visit to South America in 1947, responses to Copland's music started to shift—or rather, the associations with his Americana came to be seen as musically provincial instead of a U.S. contribution to the world of international contemporary music. The Argentinian critic Jorge d'Urbano wrote that year: "Few musical works can express with greater clarity that complex of naïveté, sentimentality, sweetness, and realism that characterizes the U.S. social environment more than *Appalachian Spring*." Like the Italian concertgoer mentioned in Bernstein's letter, Carlos Suffern—another Argentinian critic—associated *Appalachian Spring* with film music. He described the score as being "in very nice Technicolor," offering "lovely landscapes, regional songs, from the mountains, complete with pulpit and morning stars." The same association of Appalachia with America that had turned

　　　AARON COPLAND'S *APPALACHIAN SPRING*

Appalachian Spring into a symbol of the nation in the early U.S. reception now served to turn Copland into a proponent of artistic "regionalism," as the Chilean composer Juan Orrego-Salas put it in 1948. *Appalachian Spring*, Orrego-Salas wrote, was "beyond dispute a genuine expression of North America, or perhaps the most typical fruit of North American civilization." An Italian critic dubbed Copland, in a similar vein, "an American Grieg."[4]

In the United Kingdom, Copland remained present in the concert hall and on the radio as one of the musical fellow travelers of Benjamin Britten and Michael Tippett, though there too it was mostly through his 1940s Americana, in particular *Rodeo* and *Appalachian Spring*. It helped that his publisher was Boosey & Hawkes, which—in addition to its presence in New York and elsewhere—was one of the main U.K. publishing houses and thus keen to promote Copland's music. In continental Europe, however, Copland's star began to fade as quickly as it did in Latin America. In Poland and other Eastern European countries, Copland's Americana encountered polite uninterest, while German audiences of the 1950s found Copland's music "pretentious, harmless, unsatisfying, feminine, sanitized, and unbearably boring." After Copland conducted a series of concerts in Baden-Baden and elsewhere in Germany in 1955, critics found that his works were "in no way revolutionary in the contemporary sense of avant-garde new music." To German ears, Copland's music was entertainment rather than art. While these comments were entirely in line with German criticism of other neoclassical music, they are nonetheless disturbingly close to the rhetorical gist of comments against Jewish composers during the Nazi period. In Germany and elsewhere in Europe, Copland's works were soon overshadowed by the exciting contributions to new music being made by John Cage and Morton Feldman. If he was mentioned at all, it was Copland the folklorist, composing for—or pandering to—a culturally conservative audience, that pervaded and continues to pervade, European views of his works.[5]

One of the crasser examples of European responses to Copland's Americana can be found on the website of the French national radio station, Radio France. Not only does this text cast Copland as an audience pleaser—a way to feminize an artist in the world of Western music—but worse, the text implies that he did so for mere financial gain, putting him perilously close to the nadir of artistic prostitution. Thus his ballets left him a "multimillionaire by the time of his death." Yet as even this website somewhat grudgingly acknowledges, in recent years European interest in Copland and his music has started picking up. In 2011, for example, the first book on the composer in Italian was published under the title *Aaron Copland: Pioniere della musica americana* (Pioneer of American Music). The "American" label still limits the composer, but he had now become akin to the pioneer characters celebrated in *Appalachian Spring*, with American music his cultural frontier.[6]

APPALACHIAN SPRING *IN THE UNITED STATES*

In the United States, too, Copland's story was one of shifting fortunes. In 1953 he was under investigation by Senator

Joseph McCarthy's House Committee on Un-American Activities for his suspected ties to Communism. A planned performance of *Lincoln Portrait* for the inauguration of President Dwight D. Eisenhower in January that year was canceled after the Illinois Representative Fred Busby, "a strident anticommunist," protested it in a session of the House of Representatives. The composer was called to testify in a closed hearing on May 26, 1953. For Copland, who was among the most highly respected musicians in the United States, as well as one who was officially recognized during and immediately after World War II, this turn of events was potentially very damaging. Like many musicians close to the Popular Front, his social engagement was now questioned as disloyal. He had problems securing a passport, for instance, for tours abroad, and some other engagements in the United States were canceled. As often with Copland, the extent of the impact is hard to judge, but it is clear he was deeply unnerved. In 1955, when things had calmed down, he wrote *Canticle of Freedom* for chorus and orchestra. He joked in a letter to Leonard Bernstein about the title of the work: "It's called *Canticle of Freedom*. Sounds subversive, no?"[7]

Soon thereafter, however, the State Department returned to sponsoring the composer's trips as a musical ambassador for the United States: in 1960, for instance, he visited the Soviet Union and South Asia. The 1970s brought a conscious rebranding of Copland the Americanist as, for example, in a documentary that the USIA produced with the title *Copland Portrait* in 1976 for the U.S. bicentennial. The filmmaker Terry Sanders commented "that the USIA commissioned the documentary because the composer was 'such an icon of American music.'" Not only did the film recast Copland as an apolitical artist (which is quite a feat in itself), it also emphasized Copland's more modernist side by focusing on such works as his First Symphony (1924).[8]

Once Copland had been refashioned for the bicentennial as the apolitical voice of American culture, it was but a short step to appropriating his sound for Republican politics, as when Ronald Reagan's reelection campaign used the idiom associated with Copland's Americana in the "Morning in America" commercials. Alan Foust, the composer responsible for the music, remembered how he brainstormed with a colleague about the sound they tried to evoke. His colleague, "without saying anything . . . turned to the piano and (with the sustain pedal on) played C–D–G–B." While transposed, these four notes form, of course, part of the opening motif of *Appalachian Spring*. Yet Copland's score spoke equally well to Democrats. In November 1996, for instance, it was used as introductory music to Bill Clinton's victory speech in Little Rock, Arkansas.[9]

The end of the Cold War in 1989 brought yet another shift in the American construction of Copland. He died one year later, on December 2, 1990. But as scholars started to explore the role of artists during the Great Depression and the 1930s, left-leaning musicians from Copland to Marc Blitzstein garnered new appreciation; the critique of high modernism brought renewed attention to the vernacular neoclassicism of Copland and Virgil Thomson; and cultural, religious, and sexual identities became significant topics in the study of music. Copland's unabashed ownership of his American, left-wing, Jewish, and gay identities drew a great deal of attention, both scholarly and, increasingly, popular.

By the time of his centenary in 2000, Copland was perhaps the most studied and recorded American art-music
composer.

His music returned to the political stage on January 20,
2009, during the inauguration of Barack Obama as the
forty-fourth president of the United States. In the minutes
before the new president took his oath of office, a worldwide audience listened to John Williams's *Air and Simple
Gifts*, performed by a multiethnic group of four musicians: Anthony McGill (clarinet), Itzhak Perlman (violin), Yo-Yo Ma (cello), and Gabriela Montero (piano).
The Shaker tune that Copland had made so famous in
Appalachian Spring was now covered in a highly visible,
politically motivated work and served as both a homage
to the dean of American music and a celebration of musical America. At first Williams presented the famous tune
in a Coplandesque sonority and texture—with the melody
first in the clarinet and then even more emphatically in
the violin—but after that he used other vernacular idioms,
including jazz, to bring his own set of variations into the
twenty-first century.

Another politician drew on *Appalachian Spring* in a
high-profile context, in December 2011, some three years
after President Obama's inauguration. This time, however, things backfired rather dramatically. Texas Governor
Rick Perry aired a new advertisement attacking the sit-
ting president in his bid for the Republican presidential
nomination. In this short television ad, which was given
the title "Strong," Perry criticized President Obama's "war
on religion," which allowed "gays to serve in the military" whereas "our kids can't openly celebrate Christmas

or pray in school." For all its homophobic stridency, its political content was predictably unremarkable in the political climate of recent public discourse. What was noteworthy about this campaign ad, however, was its musical underscoring. Playing on familiar tropes of pastoral Americana, the music helped create an aura of wholesome Middle America.[10]

Within days after the advertisement started airing, the musical world was pouring scorn over the hapless presidential candidate and his musical advisors. "Poetic Justice," the blogger Miles Webber crowed: "Rick Perry's anti-gay ad uses music composed by a communist gay Jew." The composer in question was, of course, Aaron Copland. As quickly became clear, however, the music was not even a Copland original but—as Paul Schied put it—a "cheap knock-off" of *Appalachian Spring*. The campaign ad's music riffed on Copland's score, from the instrumentation to its melodic contour and harmonic language, but the 1944 original and its 2011 alter ego had as many differences as similarities: the modern score was far more conservative in its orchestration, and its ending delivered a bland conventionality—church bells included—that are hard to imagine flowing from the pen of so exquisite a craftsman as Copland. Yet many mistook the soundtrack for the original until the scholar and music critic Alex Ross clarified the matter for the broader public several days later on his blog, *The Rest is Noise*.[11]

The initial misattribution is a testament to the degree to which the score of *Appalachian Spring*—or some more or less precise memory of it—has by now entered the musical vocabulary of American culture. The widespread use of *Appalachian Spring* idioms—in such films as *Apollo 13* (1995), *Saving Private Ryan* (1998), *Lincoln* (2012), and *The Monuments Men* (2014)—has come to signify all things good and wholesome in American history rather than an instance of specific Coplandiana.

Graham's *Appalachian Spring,* by contrast, fared differently in U.S. reception. The choreography remained closely tied to her as a person, first as a dancer and then, when she no longer could perform the role of the Bride, her surrogates. Because of this close association between performer and role, the work as a whole became not so much a signifier for Americana (as was the case with Copland's music) as a stand-in for Graham. The choreography is to this day owned by the Martha Graham Dance Company, which still tours with it. Other dance companies may only perform Graham's choreography in a licensed production imparted by an authorized restager from the Company (a "Martha Graham Master Teacher"). Unlike other Graham choreographies, however, *Appalachian Spring* has been picked up predominantly by dance programs in high schools, colleges, and universities, rather than by professional dance companies. It prompts the question of whether this is because of the work's strong association with Graham or its musical and visual embeddedness in the cultural field of mid-century Americana.[12]

THE SHAKER TUNE TAKES OVER

As the reception of *Appalachian Spring* became increasingly dominated by the score, the work's connotations with Appalachia were overlaid with other cultural references, none more than the Shakers. In American culture, the Shakers carried dramatically changing meanings, from a ridiculed cult in the nineteenth century to the embodiment of such national values as God-fearing self-reliance. During the Great Depression Shakers drew the attention mainly of left-leaning artists and thinkers because of their communal lifestyle and artisanal products—especially furniture—with simple lines that could be instrumentalized as prototypes for American modernism. That their art intersected with worship was considered an intriguing aspect of the group's religious practice, one echoed in such works as Doris Humphrey's *Dance of the Chosen* (later titled *The Shakers*) from 1931, which presented an imagined dance service accompanied by voice, accordion, and drum. It was not until 1940 that the first major collection of Shaker music would be published: Edward D. Andrews's *The Gift to Be Simple: Songs, Dances and Rituals of the American Shakers* was a volume in the tradition of 1930s folk-song publications, with introductory notes and commentary. Because of the collection's title, all of Shaker music became immediately encapsulated in the incipit of "Simple Gifts," a song that Andrews himself considered one of the "authentic symbols of a distinct folk culture." That Copland, who had bought *The Gift to Be Simple* as soon as it was available, associated the Shakers with this particular tune might, indeed, have had to do with Andrews's title. In addition, the opening two lines of the hymn—" 'Tis the gift to be simple, 'tis the gift to be free"—would have spoken to a composer thoroughly involved in the war effort, with its constant emphasis on freedom as the key tenet of a democratic world. Yet when the work premiered in 1944, none of the critics referred to Shakers, either in terms of dance or music. Appalachia remained the main referent for several more years, and in 1948 Copland's score could still be listed as a "Humanistic treasure" that—as a musical work—could represent the Appalachian Trail.[13]

The totemic character of "Simple Gifts" with respect to *Appalachian Spring* developed slowly, and mainly through the music. An intriguing review of the Boston Symphony Orchestra's 1946 Tanglewood concerts points to Copland as the figure who originated the shift away from Graham's Appalachia toward the Shaker connotations that he clearly found more appealing, given his interest in the sect to the point of wanting to write a Shaker opera in 1941 (see chapter 1). As Jay Rosenberg wrote in his review of the concert, "Mr. Copland acknowledges his indebtedness" to Andrews, "the eminent Shaker authority" and author of *The Gift to Be Simple*, "for some of the themes which he has incorporated and developed in his composition." Rosenberg is here referring to the program note that generally accompanied performances of the suite and provided subtitles for its eight sections. Copland described the penultimate section as "Scenes of daily activity for the Bride and her Farmer-husband. There are five variations on a Shaker theme. The theme, sung by a solo clarinet, was taken from a collection of Shaker melodies compiled by Edward D. Andrews, and published under the title *The Gift to Be Simple*. The melody I borrowed and used almost literally, is called *Simple Gifts*." Such an explicit reference may have been dictated by copyright protocols, but it is nonetheless unusual for Copland: none of his other quotations—for instance, in *Billy the Kid, Lincoln Portrait,* or *Rodeo*—received this kind of acknowledgment. By the time Copland was anthologized in such compilations as *The Norton Anthology of Western Music* (1980), it was the variations on "Simple Gifts" from the *Appalachian Spring* orchestral suite that were chosen.[14]

REHISTORICIZING APPALACHIAN SPRING

While the music of *Appalachian Spring* has been appropriated as a general signifier of all things American (or Shaker), another recent development seems to move into the opposite direction, relocating the work in the specific historical context of its genesis, not only insofar as scholarship is concerned but also in terms of staging choices. Dance and music scholars alike have started to focus in detail on the ways in which Graham's choreography and Copland's score reflect cultural concerns of their time. To that end, authors such as Elizabeth Crist, Mark Franko, and Howard Pollack have followed Marta Robertson's lead, building their interpretation of the work first and foremost on Graham's "House of Victory" scenario (as well as its two later, untitled incarnations). The scenario offers a fascinating window onto the work because Graham, in an effort to communicate with the composer in Hollywood, explained to Copland in some detail not only the plot itself but also the cultural significance of her choices of characters, settings, and actions. Such documents provide the musicologist with the structure that Copland followed in his composition— with timings that coordinated with plot evolutions—while they reveal to the dance scholar how Graham developed and condensed the piece over the course of her creative process.[15]

However, Graham's initial ideas for her ballet also present a challenge to the historiography of *Appalachian Spring* because the interpretation of the work is being filtered through the prism of a set of documents that, in the end, Graham (but not Copland) discarded. As her longtime collaborator, the lighting designer Jean Rosenthal, pointed out, Graham "always began with a very literal idea, with a literal story," though this was not the endpoint, for "in their finished form, her dances are powerful abstractions, poems in motion." Yet the "literal story" has come to take the place of the dance in much recent discussion of *Appalachian Spring*, despite the fact that the story changed significantly as the choreography moved toward fruition.[16]

The turn to the context of creation also manifests itself in contemporary performances of *Appalachian Spring*. One fascinating example was a licensed performance of Graham's choreography by the Baltimore School for the Arts in 2013. What made this such an unusual enterprise was that it turned into a student research project, with the dancers and musicians making class visits to the Library of Congress. Seeing and touching Copland's autograph score and Graham's letters helped immerse the young performers in the specificity of historical research in the arts. The *Washington Post*, riffing on the work's plot, lauded the initiative under the headline "Young Baltimore Dancers Are Pioneers in *Appalachian Spring*." This project can be inscribed, of course, in the greater enterprise of historically informed performance practice that we mostly associate with the staging of baroque opera but has recently expanded to later repertoire, yet it does take on a slightly different slant in relation to a copyright-protected choreography. In an ironic twist, the students' historical work of reconstruction helped complete the more presentist enterprise of licensed restaging into a new whole, bringing music, dance, and scenery together in a reenactment of a historical event with contemporary bodies. This is particularly poignant when a young Asian American dancer identified as much with Yuriko—who had created her role in 1944—as with the character of the Follower.[17]

The opposite happened in 2011 when Minou Lallemand rechoreographed *Appalachian Spring* for the Onium Ballet Project in Hawaii. The company's website announces that it was "a new version of the iconic American ballet, *Appalachian Spring*," a fascinating slippage because it identified the ballet with Copland's score rather than Graham's choreography (which, of course, cannot have a new version by a different choreographer). Lallemand based her decision to create a new choreography, set during World War II, on the fact that during the composition Copland "never had Appalachia in mind at all." Instead, "*Appalachian Spring* was written during World War II. So I came up with this story of this family and the soldier who has to go off to war, and the wife and family is left behind." Lallemand chose to choreograph the work in a classical-ballet style rather than a modern-dance one. This decision distanced the new version of *Appalachian Spring* as far as possible from Graham's dance, for all that Graham's choreography remained vivid as an intertext in the minds of the audience.

Lallemand's choice to set the choreography in the time period of the work's composition is, of course, in close alignment with recent staging trends that locate theatrical and operatic works in the period of their creation rather than the one they nominally represent (as occurred in the 2015 Santa Fe Opera productions of Giuseppe Verdi's *Rigoletto* and Richard Strauss's *Salome*). In the case of Lallemand's new choreography of *Appalachian Spring,* moving the plot into World War II can be seen as a search for authenticity of a different kind from that of the reenactment in Baltimore.[18]

Both the 2011 Hawaii production and John Williams's reworking of *Appalachian Spring* for the presidential inauguration in 2009 as *Air and Simple Gifts* reveal that the score's afterlife has split dramatically from the preservation of Graham's choreography in its licensed staging. Even if the latter fluctuates with each performative iteration, just as Graham was prepared to adapt the work to the abilities of her dancers, the choreography, in the end, remains—by artistic necessity and in accordance with copyright law—frozen within a very circumscribed horizon of interpretation. The 1958 film and the widespread distribution of the photographs from the first production have also contributed to treating the choreography as a static artifact that must by its very nature resist change. In contrast, Copland's music has cycled through a number of versions that are performed, recorded, and broadcast around the world. This has created a malleability that could reduce the work into a sonic signature, to be borrowed and transformed at will. It has also, however, allowed the score to move almost seamlessly between historic reconstruction—in the Baltimore School for the

Arts production—and recomposition, as when Williams remodeled the Shaker variations through the filter of contemporary popular music. As for *Appalachian Spring* in its many iterations over time, the fixed choreography, the fluid score, and even our historical accounts of the first performance on October 30, 1944, and its consequences have served to define a keynote work of American modernist music and dance.

ADDITIONAL SOURCES FOR READING AND LISTENING

ONE OF THE MOST important documents of *Appalachian Spring* is the 1958 film that was reissued on DVD, with a rich cache of additional material, by Criterion as *Martha Graham: Dance on Film* (2007). There is also useful visual and other information at the Library of Congress in Washington, D.C., which has digitized a remarkable range of documents pertaining to *Appalachian Spring* and its genesis (http://www. loc.gov). The Library of Congress also published two articles by Wayne Shirley on the creation of the work in a richly illustrated and documented booklet, *Ballet for Martha & Ballets for Martha* (Washington, DC: Library of Congress, 1997). Though less easily accessible, Marta Elaine Robertson's doctoral dissertation, "'A Gift to Be Simple': The Collaboration of Aaron Copland and Martha Graham in the Genesis of *Appalachian Spring*" (University of Michigan, 1992) presents a wealth of primary sources in her multifaceted discussion of the work's creation.

Most scholarship about *Appalachian Spring* has approached the work either from the perspective of the composer or by focusing on the choreographer. Mark Franko shows how Graham's work in *Appalachian Spring* relates to her political and biographical concerns in *Martha Graham in Love and War: The Life in the Work* (New York: Oxford University Press, 2012). Howard Pollack's very thoroughly researched biography, *Aaron Copland: The Life and Work of an Uncommon Man* (Urbana: University of Illinois Press, 1999) offers an excellent overview of the work's genesis. Elizabeth B. Crist interprets *Appalachian Spring* in the context of Copland's affinity for the Popular Front in *Music for the Common Man: Aaron Copland during the Depression and War* (Oxford and New York: Oxford University Press, 2005). Aaron Copland's autobiography, cowritten with Vivian Perlis, presents a fascinating and lively retrospective, supplemented with comments from such dancers as Erick Hawkins, Pearl Lang, and May O'Donnell (*Copland since 1943* [New York: St. Martin's Press, 1989], reprinted in *The Complete Copland* [Hillsdale, NY: Pendragon Press, 2012]).

A number of books provide further context. My own *Sounds of War: Music in the United States during World War II* (New York: Oxford University Press, 2013) discusses American concert music, including *Appalachian Spring*, from 1939 to 1945. Lynn Garafola frames the Copland-Graham collaboration in the context of Copland's earlier American ballets in her essay "Making an American Dance: *Billy the Kid, Rodeo,* and *Appalachian Spring*," in *Aaron Copland and His World*, edited by Carol J. Oja and Judith Tick (Princeton, NJ: Princeton University Press, 2005). Julia L. Foulkes, *Modern Bodies: Dance and American Modernism from Martha Graham to Alvin Ailey* (Chapel Hill: University of North Carolina Press, 2002), discusses the work in the context of modern dance. Finally, to contextualize the debate about Appalachia's role in American culture, the classic study by Allen W. Batteau, *The Invention of Appalachia* (Tucson: University of Arizona Press, 1990), still presents one of the most pertinent introductions to how Appalachia came to be "a creature of the urban imagination" (p. 1).

NOTES

INTRODUCTION

1 Aaron Copland, letter to Darius Milhaud, June 19, 1944, Darius Milhaud Collection, Paul Sacher Stiftung (Americana); I am grateful to Erin K. Maher for sharing this letter with me. Copland cited in Howard Pollack, *Aaron Copland: The Life and Work of an Uncommon Man* (Urbana: University of Illinois Press, 1999), 402 (spring).

2 Erick Hawkins, letter to Harold Spivacke, October 3, 1944, Library of Congress, Old Music Division Correspondence, reproduced in Aaron Copland and Vivian Perlis, *Aaron Copland since 1943* (New York: St. Martin's Press, 1989), 34.

3 Elizabeth B. Crist, *Music for the Common Man: Aaron Copland during the Depression and War* (Oxford and New York: Oxford University Press, 2005), 165–76; and Mark Franko, *Martha Graham in Love and War: The Life in the Work* (New York: Oxford University Press, 2012), 15–64.

4 Summary based on Pollack, *Aaron Copland*, 388–403. See also the detailed overview of the commission in Marta Elaine Robertson, "'A Gift to Be Simple': The Collaboration of Aaron Copland and Martha Graham in the Genesis of *Appalachian Spring*" (Ph.D. diss., University of Michigan, 1992), 127–51.

5 Copland and Perlis, *Copland since 1943*, 34 (surprise); Aaron Copland, letter to Darius Milhaud, June 19, 1944, Darius Milhaud Collection, Paul Sacher Stiftung (Graham-iana); and Program for the Tenth Festival of Chamber Music, Washington, DC, Coolidge Auditorium, October 28–30, 1944, *MGC*, box 321 (plot summary).

6 On the physicality of Graham's authorship, see Anthea Kraut, *Choreographing Copyright: Race, Gender, and Intellectual Property Rights in American Dance* (New York: Oxford University Press, 2016), 248.

7 See http://www.merriam-webster.com/dictionary/locavore and http://www.nytimes.com/2013/04/21/arts/music/orpheus-to-play-kahanes-gabriels-

guide-to-48-states.html. On left-wing populism, see Morris Dickstein, *Dancing in the Dark: A Cultural History of the Great Depression* (New York: Norton, 2009), 462. Constance Rourke (1933), cited in Michael C. Steiner, "Introduction: Varieties of Western American Regionalism," in *Regionalists on the Left: Radical Voices from the American West*, ed. Steiner (Norman: University of Oklahoma Press, 2013), 1–20, 12.

8 Seeger (1943), cited in Benjamin Filene, *Romancing the Folk: Public Memory and American Roots Music* (Chapel Hill: University of North Carolina Press, 2000), 151.

9 Filene, *Romancing the Folk*, 155–57.

10 Tim Carter, *"Oklahoma!" The Making of an American Musical* (New Haven, CT: Yale University Press, 2007).

11 Lynn Garafola, "Lincoln Kirstein, Modern Dance, and the Left: The Genesis of an American Ballet," *Dance Research* 23 (2005): 18–35; W. E. B. Du Bois, cited in Franko, *Martha Graham in Love and War*, 60–61 (Appalachian range); on Appalachia, see Allen W. Batteau, *The Invention of Appalachia* (Tucson: University of Arizona Press, 1990); on the Soviet use of folk dance, see Ellen Graff, *Stepping Left: Dance and Politics in New York City, 1928–1942* (Durham, NC: Duke University Press, 1997), 132–52.

12 I. M. J. [Isabel Morse Jones], "Aaron Copland Scores with Music of Russia," *Los Angeles Times*, May 30, 1943 (all-American composer). In a letter to Carlos Chávez dated March 3, 1943, Copland emphasized the film's "Russian" character; see Copland, *The Selected Correspondence of Aaron Copland*, ed. Elizabeth B. Crist and Wayne Shirley (New Haven, CT: Yale University Press, 2006), 150.

13 Margaret Lloyd, "Poetic Imagery in Movement," *Christian Science Monitor*, February 10, 1945 (small house); and Sam Hood, "*Appalachian Spring*: Martha Graham Film Held Over Here," *Pittsburgh Press*, January 15, 1959 (Appalachian). On Graham's tours, see Victoria Phillips Geduld, "Dancing Diplomacy: Martha Graham and the Strange Commodity of Cold-War Cultural Exchange in Asia, 1955 and 1974," *Dance Chronicle* 33 (2010): 44–81.

CHAPTER 1

1 The citations from Martha Graham stem from the following letters: to Elizabeth Sprague Coolidge, November 4, 1942, in Wayne D. Shirley, *Ballet for Martha: The Commissioning of "Appalachian Spring"; and, Ballets for Martha: The Creation of "Appalachian Spring," "Jeux de Printemps," and "Hérodiade"* (Washington, DC: Library of Congress, 1989), 14; and to Aaron Copland, May 16 and July 10, 1943, *ACC*, box 255, folder 22. See also William Carlos Williams, "War, the Destroyer!," *Harper's Bazaar*, March 1, 1942, 49.

2 Martha Graham, letters to Aaron Copland, May 16, July 10, and September 5, 1943, as well as an undated letter also from 1943, *ACC*, box 255, folder 22; and Aaron Copland, letter to Martha Graham, ca. July 20, 1943, copied as an extract in Martha Graham, letter to Harold Spivacke, July 27, 1943, *ESCC*, box 36, folder 5.

3 Erick Hawkins, letter to Elizabeth Sprague Coolidge, May 21, 1942, *EHC*, box 56 (creative artists); Elizabeth Sprague Coolidge, letters to Erick Hawkins, May 29 and June 16, 1942, *EHC*, box 53; and Erick Hawkins, letter to Elizabeth Sprague Coolidge, August 4, 1942, *EHC*, box 56 (new lease).

4 Martha Graham, letter to Elizabeth Sprague Coolidge, August 12, 1942, *ESCC*, box 36.

5 On the role of the Gettysburg Address during World War II, see Barry Schwartz, "Memory as a Cultural System: Abraham Lincoln in World War II," *American Sociological Review* 61 (1996): 908–27. Quotations from Aaron Copland in letter to Benjamin Britten, summer 1942, reproduced in Aaron Copland and Vivian Perlis, *Copland: 1900 through 1942* (New York: St. Martin's Press, 1984), 364–65 (frothy ballet); and Alfred Frankenstein, "*Rodeo* Is Refreshing and as American as Mark Twain," *San Francisco Chronicle*, November 20, 1942 (Mark Twain). See also Annegret Fauser, *Sounds of War: Music in the United States during World War II* (New York: Oxford University Press, 2013), 21–22; and Crist, *Music for the Common Man*, 146–91.

6 Quotations from Aaron Copland, letter to Arthur Berger, April 10, 1943, in "Aaron Copland and Arthur Berger in Correspondence," ed. and introd. Wayne D. Shirley, in *Aaron Copland and His World*, ed. Carol J. Oja and Judith Tick (Princeton, NJ: Princeton University Press, 2005), 191 (naturalness); and Roger Sessions, "On the American Future" (1940), in *Roger Sessions on Music: Collected Essays*, ed. Edward T. Cone (Princeton, NJ: Princeton University Press, 1979), 289–90 (quasi-fascist). See also Crist, *Music for the Common Man*, 86; and Graff, *Stepping Left*, 133–34.

7 Ted Shawn's comment to Agnes de Mille is given in Copland and Perlis, *Copland: 1900 through 1942*, 359.

8 Quotations from Martha Graham, interview with Marcia Minor, "Graham Interprets Democracy," *Daily Worker*, October 7, 1938, in "American Document," *Performing Arts Encyclopedia*, Library of Congress, accessed July 21, 2014, http://www.loc.gov/item/ihas.200182818 (rights); and "Dance Libretto: *American Document*, by Martha Graham," *Theatre Arts* 26 (September 1942): 565 (listening). Information about *American Document* and on Graham as a celebrity drawn from Franko, *Martha Graham in Love and War*, 14–44 and 66–74.

9 Franko, *Martha Graham in Love and War*, 28–30; and Martin Duberman, *The Worlds of Lincoln Kirstein* (New York: Alfred A. Knopf, 2007), 315–20.

10 On Copland's interest in a Shaker-themed one-act opera, see Edwin Denby, letter to Aaron Copland (1941), cited in Pollack, *Aaron Copland*, 639n39; and Lincoln Kirstein, "Memorial Day: Dances for a Democracy in Crisis" (1938), typescript ballet scenario, *ACC*, box 228. Quotations are, in sequence, from Erick Hawkins, letter to Elizabeth Sprague Coolidge, [October 1942], *EHC*, box 56 (carbon copy) and Library of Congress, Old Music Division Correspondence (all set); and Martha Graham, letter to Aaron Copland, November 7, 1942, *ACC*, box 255, folder 22 (working). Lynn Garafola mentions "Memorial Day" in connection with *Appalachian Spring* in "Making an American Dance: *Billy the Kid, Rodeo,* and *Appalachian Spring,*" in *Aaron Copland and His World*, 121–47 and 136.

11 All quotations from Kirstein, "Memorial Day," scenario.

12 Quotations, in sequence, from Kirstein, "Memorial Day," scenario (industry), and Martha Graham, undated letter to Lincoln Kirstein, written from Washington, DC, Lincoln Kirstein Papers, Jerome Robbins Dance Division, New York Public Library, *MGZMD 97, box 6, folder 102 (outlines); the letter is cited in part and discussed in Garafola, "Lincoln Kirstein, Modern Dance, and the Left," 22.

13 This and the following two paragraphs refer to and quote from Martha Graham, "House of Victory" (1943), typescript ballet scenario, *ACC*, box 255, folder 22.

14 On Graham and *Oklahoma!*, see Agnes de Mille, *Martha: The Life and Works of Martha Graham* (New York: Random House, 1991), 264. Citations from Graham, "House of Victory," scenario.

15 For time of completion, see Harold Spivacke, letter to Martha Graham, May 3, 1943, *ESCC*, box 36; quotation from Martha Graham, letter to Aaron Copland, May 16, 1943, *ACC*, box 255, folder 22. The main four collections with correspondence about *Appalachian Spring* are all at the Library of Congress: *ACC, EHC, ESCC,* and *MGC.*

16 Quotations are, in sequence, from Martha Graham, letters to Aaron Copland, May 29 and July 10, 1943; Martha Graham, "Name?" (second typescript scenario, 1943); and Martha Graham, undated letter to Aaron Copland, [after July 10, 1943]; all *ACC*, box 255, folder 22.

CHAPTER 2

1 Quotations from Aaron Copland, untitled and undated note about *The North Star, ACC,* box 407 (guided); and from I. M. J. [Isabel Morse Jones],"Aaron Copland Scores with Music of Russia," *Los Angeles Times*, May 30, 1943 (all-American). For an overview of Copland's contribution to *The North Star*, see Pollack, *Aaron Copland*, 378–83.

2 Quotations from Copland, *The North Star* (note) (Schostakovitch), and from Aaron Copland, letter to Leonard Bernstein, September 14, 1943, *LBC*, box 16 (numbers). In his note on *The North Star*, Copland spells 'Tis as T'Is.

3 On Hammerstein in the context of mainstreaming, see Andrea Most, *Making Americans: Jews and the Broadway Musical* (Cambridge, MA: Harvard University Press, 2004). On Boulanger, Copland, and national identity, see Annegret Fauser, "Aaron Copland, Nadia Boulanger, and the Making of an 'American' Composer," *Musical Quarterly* 89 (2006): 524–55. For Copland's linking of identity and subconscious choice, see, for example, his letter to Leonard Bernstein (1939), cited in Pollack, *Aaron Copland*, 522–23.

4 Copland on American and Jewish qualities cited in Pollack, *Aaron Copland*, 523; longer extract from Copland and Perlis, *Copland: 1900 through 1942*, 16.

5 The musical observations are based on the brief analysis of the film score and the sonata in Pollack, *Aaron Copland*, 382–85. Julia Smith connects the musical language of the sonata with *Appalachian Spring* in *Aaron Copland: His Work and Contribution to American Music* (New York: E. P. Dutton, 1955), 235.

6 Quotations, in sequence, from Aaron Copland, letter to Leonard Bernstein (undated, late spring 1943), *LBC*, box 16 (dull); and Aaron Copland, letter to Martha Graham (ca. July 20, 1943), copied as an extract in Martha Graham, letter to Harold Spivacke, July 27, 1943, *ESCC*, box 36, folder 5 (sketched).

7 Martha Graham, letter to Erick Hawkins, July 27, 1943, *EHC*, box 55, folder 3. Chávez did finally send his score in July 1945. Graham choreographed it as *Dark Meadow*; it was premiered on January 23, 1946.

8 Aaron Copland, datebook 1943, entry for October 22: "2.30 pm Martha Graham," *ACC*, box 233. The quotations are, in sequence, from Martha Graham, letter to Harold Spivacke, undated but stamped October 27, 1943, *ESCC*, box 36, folder 2 (joy); and Martha Graham, letter to Aaron Copland, August 5, 1944, *ACC*, box 255, folder 22 (cursing). On the relationship between the final choreography and the earlier scripts, see Franko, *Martha Graham in Love and War*, 45–65.

9 Yuriko and Osato are discussed in Carol J. Oja, *Bernstein Meets Broadway: Collaborative Art in a Time of War* (New York: Oxford University Press, 2014), 138–39.

10 On Arch Lauterer, see Don McDonagh, *Martha Graham: A Biography* (New York: Praeger, 1973), 176; Erick Hawkins is quoted in Copland and Perlis, *Copland since 1943*, 39. On Noguchi's concept of hybridity, see Amy Lyford, "Noguchi, Sculptural Abstraction, and the politics of Japanese American Internment," *Art Bulletin* 85 (2003): 137–51, esp. 141. For Langston Hughes, see Fauser, *Sounds of War*, 232.

11 Noguchi's drawings were first published in Gail Levin and Judith Tick, *Aaron Copland's America: A Cultural Perspective* (New York: Watson-Guptill, 2000), 103; Hawkins cited in Laurie Schwab '46, "Hawkins Defines Essence of Martha Graham Technique," *Vassar Miscellany News*, January 24, 1945; Yuriko cited in Robert Tracy, *Goddess: Martha Graham's Dancers Remember* (New York: Limelight Editions, 1997), 107; and on the association of the fence with internment camps, see Marta Robertson, "American Music as Diasporic Process: From Internment Camps to *Appalachian Spring*," paper presented at the Annual Meeting of the Society for American Music, Pittsburgh, PA, March 2007.

12 Anna Sokolow, cited in de Mille, *Martha*, 148 (girls); Martha Graham, undated letter to Aaron Copland, *ACC*, box 255, folder 22 (legend).

13 One example of the conflation among many is Helen Thomas, *Dance, Modernity, and Culture: Explorations in the Sociology of Dance* (London and New York: Routledge, 1995), 144–45; de Mille, *Martha*, 262 (rapt ecstasy); 1955 program note cited in Franko, *Martha Graham in Love and War*, 57 (fanatic); Erick Hawkins, undated letter to Martha Graham, *EHC*, box 55, folder 3 (his part). On choreography, see Robertson, " 'A Gift to Be Simple,' " 222–23.

14 Harold Spivacke, letter to Darius Milhaud, April 25, 1944, in Shirley, *Ballet for Martha*, 46 (dances); Erick Hawkins, letter to Harold Spivacke, August 27, 1944, Library of Congress, Old Music Division Correspondence (third). Financial information on *Carmen Jones*, see Annegret Fauser, " 'Dixie *Carmen*': War, Race, and Identity in Oscar Hammerstein's *Carmen Jones* (1943)," *Journal of the Society for American Music* 4 (2010): 146.

15 Erick Hawkins, letter to Harold Spivacke, October 3, 1944; quotation from Harold Spivacke, letter to Martha Graham, October 5, 1944, both Library of Congress, Old Music Division Correspondence.

16 Martha Graham, letter to Aaron Copland, August 12, 1942, *ACC*, box 255, folder 22. Quotations from Martha Graham, letter to Harold Spivacke, undated but stamped October 27, 1943, *ESCC*, box 36, folder 2 (worry); and Martha Graham, letter to Aaron Copland, June 19, 1944, *ACC*, box 255, folder 22 (expense). On the draft, see Harold Spivacke, letter to Martha Graham, June 21, 1944, *ESCC*, box 36, folder 3.

17 Erick Hawkins, letter to Harold Spivacke, September 22, 1944, Library of Congress, Old Music Division Correspondence (union); Aaron Copland, letter for Leonard Bernstein, October 9, 1944, *LBC*, box 16 (Graham); and John Martin, "The Dance: Busy Days Ahead," *New York Times*, October 8, 1944 (nothing). On Spivacke, see Fauser, *Sounds of War*, 76–134; and on Austin-Wilder, see Robertson, " 'A Gift to Be Simple,' " 151.

CHAPTER 3

1 The key text addressing the work concept in Western music is Lydia Goehr, *The Imaginary Museum of Musical Works* (Oxford and New York: Oxford University Press, 1992); for a recent discussion, see Mark Evan Bonds, *Absolute Music: The History of an Idea* (New York: Oxford University Press, 2014).

2 On Martha Graham's legal rights as choreographer and copyright issues in dance more generally, see Kraut, *Choreographing Copyright*; Robertson, "'A Gift to Be Simple,'" 207–92; and Marta Robertson, "Musical and Choreographic Integration of Copland's and Graham's 'Appalachian Spring,'" *Musical Quarterly* 83 (1999): 6–26.

3 On Graham's rechoreographing, see Victoria Thoms, *Martha Graham: Gender and the Haunting of a Dance Pioneer* (Bristol and Chicago: Intellect, 2013), 12; see also the comparisons between the original version and the 1958 film by Deborah Jowitt (DVD 1) and in "The Dancers" (DVD 2), *Martha Graham: Dance on Film* (Criterion Collection DVDs, 2007).

4 Program for the Tenth Festival of Chamber Music, Washington, D.C., Coolidge Auditorium, October 28–30, 1944, *MGC*, box 321 (part and parcel); and Blase Washington, "*Appalachian Spring* . . . A Dance of Life," *Mayfair*, December 1944, 42 (shining).

5 Pearl Lang, cited in Copland and Perlis, *Copland since 1943*, 42.

6 Edwin Denby, "The Dance: *Appalachian Spring*," *New York Herald Tribune*, May 15, 1945 (striking).

7 Costume colors are described in Washington, "*Appalachian Spring* . . . A Dance of Life."

8 Aaron Copland, interview with Phillip Ramey (1974), cited in Robertson, "'A Gift to Be Simple,'" 194. My reading of the opening is deeply indebted to Stanley Kleppinger, "A Contextually Defined Approach to *Appalachian Spring*," *Indiana Theory Review* 27 (2009): 45–78, though Kleppinger's comments about timbre refer to the orchestral suite, not the dance score. For a description of pastoral idioms in Copland's musical vocabulary see Neil Lerner, "Copland's Music of Wide Open Spaces: Surveying the Pastoral Trope in Hollywood," *Musical Quarterly* 85 (2001): 483–84.

9 Several newspaper articles indicate this sequence of characters entering the stage. It differs from the 1958 filmed choreography and the rehearsal score (*MGC*, box 10), which have the Followers arriving last. See, for example, Lloyd, "Poetic Imagery in Movement," and Washington, "*Appalachian Spring* . . . A Dance of Life."

10 Stuart Hodes, in the interview released on DVD 2 of *Martha Graham: Dance on Film*, explains that the film's movements are out of sync with the music here and demonstrates how dance and score relate in the choreography.

11 Quotations from Lloyd, "Poetic Imagery in Movement" (joy); and John Martin, "Washington Festival," *New York Times*, November 5, 1944 (radiant).

12 These quotations are taken, in sequence, from the following three reviews: Lloyd, "Poetic Imagery in Movement"; Louis Biancolli, "The Dance: Copland-Graham Ballet Blends Best of Two Arts," *New York World Telegram*, May 15, 1945; and Edwin Denby, "Martha Graham Notes," *New York Herald Tribune*, May 20, 1945.

13 Aaron Copland, *Appalachian Spring (Ballet for Martha)* (New York: Boosey & Hawkes, 1945).

14 Robertson details these changes in "'A Gift to Be Simple,'" 273–78.

15 On Stravinsky, see, for example, Olin Downes, "Rodzinski Offers Music of Copland," *New York Times*, October 5, 1945; and Irving Kolodin, "Philharmonic Is 104; Rodzinski Opens Season in Carnegie—Copland Score Applauded," *New York Sun*, October 5, 1945. Copland told Irving Fine in a letter dated May 7, 1945 (*ACC*), that he "managed to complete the slow movement of the Symph." while having "also just about finished a Suite from *Appalachian Spring* for orchestra of normal proportions."

16 Janet Eilber, telephone interview with the author, September 4, 2015.

CHAPTER 4

1 Quotations from Martha Graham, "Name?" (1943), typescript scenario, *ACC*, box 255, folder 22.

2 Martha Graham, cited in "Purely Symbolic," *Time*, May 28, 1945, 62.

3 George Beiswanger, "Martha Graham: Three New Dances," *Theatre Arts* 29 (January 1945): 52 (spring); Miles Kastendieck, "Martha Graham Introduces *Appalachian Spring* in Opening at the National," *Brooklyn Eagle*, May 15, 1945 (symbolic); and Robert A. Hague, "Graham Dances Pioneer Spring," *PM*, May 15, 1945 (frontier).

4 R. S. S., "Moderns in Review," *Dance*, June 1945 (daring); and Artur Michel, "Amerikanischer Frühling," *Aufbau* (May 18, 1945): 10; http://archive.org/stream/aufbau111945germ#page/n313/mode/1up) (*uramerikanisches Werk*).

5 John Martin, "Graham Dances in Festival Finale," *New York Times*, November 1, 1944. On the frontier in American music, see Beth Ellen Levy, *Frontier Figures: American Music and the Mythology of the American West, 1895–1945* (Berkeley and Los Angeles: University of California Press, 2012).

6 NBC Shortwave Monitoring Service, "Transcript of Talk Addressed to Martha Graham by the German Radio. Speaker Is Dr. Otto Koishwitz" (June 15, 1941), *MGC*, box 318. For the second Koischwitz extract, see also Franko, *Martha Graham in Love and War*, 67.

7 Robert Sabin, "Dance at the Coolidge Festival," *Dance Observer* 11 (December 1944): 121 (throne); and Claudia Cassidy, "Martha Graham and Aaron Copland Good Companions in Superb *Appalachian Spring*," *Chicago Tribune*, March 18, 1946 (close).

8 Lloyd, "Poetic Imagery in Movement."

9 Denby, "The Dance: *Appalachian Spring*."

10 The use of the western as a genre offers one fascinating example in this context. See Christine Bold, *The Frontier Club: Popular Westerns and Cultural Power, 1880–1924* (New York: Oxford University Press, 2013); on Maslow's *Dust Bowl Ballads*, see Graff, *Stepping Left*, 139–47; Graham's comment on Maslow cited in Geduld, "Dancing Diplomacy," 44–81, 65; for Siegmeister, see Fauser, *Sounds of War*, 151–55; and reference to "shoutin' preacher" (and earlier, in the same text "shoutin' parson") in Beiswanger, "Martha Graham: Three New Dances."

11 Horace Grenell, "Copland's *Appalachian Spring* Danced by Martha Graham," *Daily Worker*, May 19, 1945 (America); Kastendieck, "Martha Graham Introduces *Appalachian Spring*" (ordinary); and Edwin Denby, "Martha Graham Notes," *New York Herald Tribune*, May 20, 1945 (isolation).

12 The press lists for the Washington premiere are reproduced in Robertson, "'A Gift to Be Simple,'" 151–52nn88–89. The net cast to capture any reference to *Appalachian Spring* between October 1944 and November 1945 included a number of databases such as Proquest Historical Newspapers and Readex African-American newspapers, 1827–1998, as well as the clippings in both *ACC* and *MGC*.

13 Michael Denning, *The Cultural Front: The Laboring of American Culture in the Twentieth Century* (London and New York: Verso, 1996); and Fauser, *Sounds of War*.

14 On the blurring of boundaries between modern dance and ballet, see Julia L. Foulkes, *Modern Bodies: Dance and American Modernism from Martha Graham to Alvin Ailey* (Chapel Hill: University of North Carolina Press, 2002), 154–55; see also Garafola, "Making an American Dance," 139–40.

15 Louis Biancolli, "The Dance: Copland-Graham Ballet Blends Best of Two Arts," *New York World Telegram*, May 15, 1945 (healthy); "Moderns in Review," *Dance*, June 1945 (pas de deux); Lloyd, "Poetic Imagery in Movement" (ballet); Sabin, "Dance at the Coolidge Festival," 121 (transparent); and "Purely Symbolic," 62 (newest).

16 Warren Storey Smith, "Symphony Concert," *Boston Post*, October 6, 1945 (truly American); Rudolph Elie, Jr., "Sunday Symphony," *Boston Herald*, October 22, 1945 (naïve).

CHAPTER 5

1 "It Happens in the World of Music," *New York Times*, May 19, 1946 (Vienna); and Leonard Bernstein, letter to Aaron Copland, May 16, 1948, in Copland and Perlis, *Copland since 1943*, 48 (success).

2 On U.S. musical diplomacy during World War II, see Fauser, *Sounds of War*, 94–105.

3 Quotations and information from Geduld, "Dancing Diplomacy," 44–81; and final quotation from Naima Prevots, *Dance for Export: Cultural Diplomacy and the Cold War* (Middletown, CT: Wesleyan University Press, 1998), 47. While Geduld and Prevots focus on *Appalachian Spring*, Clare Croft emphasizes the other works (such as *Phaedra*) during the 1974 tour in *Dancers as Diplomats: American Choreography in Cultural Exchange* (New York: Oxford University Press, 2015), 105–42.

4 Jorge d'Urbano, "Aaron Copland dirigió un concierto de sus obras anoche en el T. Colón" (1947) (musical works); and Carlos Suffern, "Conciertos" (Technicolor), both given in translation in Carol A. Hess, "Copland in Argentina: Pan Americanist Politics, Folklore, and the Crisis in Modern Music," *Journal of the American Musicological Society* 66 (2013): 225 and 228. Juan Orrego-Salas, "Aaron Copland: A New York Composer," *Tempo*, n.s. 9 (Autumn 1948): 16 (regionalism); and press digest for "Korn Concert at Opera, Italy," *ACC*, box 394 (American Grieg).

5 The information on the Polish reception was offered by my colleague Andrea Bohlman. I am very grateful for her generous sharing of unpublished research. On Germany, see Amy C. Beal, *New Music, New Allies: American Experimental Music in West Germany from the Zero Hour to Reunification* (Berkeley and Los Angeles: University of California Press, 2006), 76–77.

6 "Aaron Copland," accessed September 28, 2014, http://www.francemusique. fr/personne/aaron-copland; Luciano Feliciani, *Aaron Copland: Pioniere della musica Americana* (Varese: Zecchini Editore, 2011).

7 Pollack, *Aaron Copland*, 452–59 and, on *Canticle of Freedom*, 479–80. Quotation from Copland's letter to Leonard Bernstein (April 3, 1955) in Copland and Perlis, *Copland since 1943*, 231.

8 On the trip to the USSR, see Kevin Bartig, "Aaron Copland's Soviet Diary (1960)," *Notes* 70 (2014): 575–96; and on *Copland Portrait*, see Emily Abrams Ansari, "Aaron Copland and the Politics of Cultural Diplomacy," *Journal of the Society for American Music* 6 (2011): 355.

9 On the Reagan campaign, see Alex Ross, *The Rest Is Noise: Listening to the Twentieth Century* (New York: Farrar, Straus & Giroux, 2007), 277; and Ross, "Composing Reagan," *The Rest Is Noise* (blog), September 15, 2007, accessed September 22, 2014, http://www.therestisnoise.com/2007/09/composing-morni.html. On the use of *Appalachian Spring* in 1996, see Lerner, "Copland's Music of Wide Open Spaces," 501.

10 Advertisement, "Strong" (December 6, 2011), accessed September 21, 2014, https://www.youtube.com/watch?v=0PAJNntoRgA.

11 Miles Webber, "Poetic Justice: Rick Perry's Anti-Gay Ad Uses Music Composed by a Communist Gay Jew," NeoGAF, December 11, 2011, http:// www.neogaf.com/forum/showthread.php?p=33376045; Paul Schied, "A Strong Response," *Harvard Political Review*, December 9, 2011, http://harvardpolitics.

com/united-states/a-strong-response; and Alex Ross, "Copland and the Republicans," *The Rest is Noise* (blog), December 10, 2011, http://www.therestisnoise.com/2011/12/copland-and-the-republicans.html; all three accessed September 21, 2014.

12 Janet Eilber, telephone interview with the author, September 4, 2015; see also information about licensing at http://marthagraham.org/licensing/, accessed September 12, 2015.

13 Edward D. Andrews, *The Gift to Be Simple: Songs, Dances and Rituals of the American Shakers* (New York: Dover, 1940), 7 and 136 (authentic); and from Louise Elder, "Appalachian Trail" (letter to the editor), *Springfield Republican*, May 30, 1948 (Humanistic). On "Simple Gifts," see also William Brooks, "Simple Gifts and Complex Accretions," in *Copland Connotations: Studies and Interviews*, ed. Peter Dickinson (Woodbridge and Rochester, NY: Boydell, 2002), 103–17.

14 Jay C. Rosenfeld, "20,000 Attend Two Concerts at Tanglewood Over Week End," *Berkshire Evening Eagle*, July 29, 1946 (indebtedness); Aaron Copland, Program Note for *Appalachian Spring*, New York Philharmonic Orchestra, October 4, 1945, program digitized at http://archives.nyphil.org/index.php/artifact/07d9bc56-1829-44f3-920d-33dad1d4edd7/fullview#page/6/mode/2up, accessed September 14, 2015 (scenes); and Claude V. Palisca, ed., *The Norton Anthology of Western Music* (New York: Norton, 1980).

15 Crist, *Music for the Common Man*, 167–76; Franko, *Martha Graham in Love and War*, 45–65; Pollack, *Aaron Copland*, 393–403; and Robertson, "'A Gift to Be Simple,'" chapters 4–6.

16 Jean Rosenthal and Lael Wertenbaker, *The Magic of Light: The Craft and Career of Jean Rosenthal, Pioneer in Lighting for the Modern Stage* (Boston: Little, Brown, 1972), 129.

17 Rebecca Ritzel, "Young Baltimore Dancers Are Pioneers in *Appalachian Spring*," *Washington Post*, April 5, 2013; for a short report as well as a video produced by the students that contains interviews with the performers, see http://blogs.loc.gov/music/2013/04/an-appalachian-spring-collaboration/?loclr=blogtea. Another such project in the context of U.S. higher education is the staging of *Oklahoma!* at the North Carolina School for the Arts in 2011; see http://www.uncsa.edu/performances/OKwebisodes.htm, accessed September 14, 2015.

18 See "*Appalachian Spring*: Onium Ballet Project," http://www.hawaiiconcertsociety.com/oniumballet.html; and Steven Mark, "Copland Revisited in New Choreography of *Appalachian Spring*," *Honolulu Star-Advertiser*, February 25, 2011, http://www.honolulupulse.com/2011/02/copland-revisited-in-a-new-choreography-of-appalachian-spring/, both accessed September 14, 2015.

INDEX